ANTI-TANK WEAPONS

Brassey's *Modern Military Equipment*

ANTI-TANK WEAPONS

John Norris

First English Edition 1996

UK editorial offices: Brassey's, 33 John Street, London WC1N 2AT
UK orders: Marston Book Services, PO Box 269, Abingdon, OX14 4SD

North American orders: Brassey's Inc., PO Box 960,
Herndon, VA 22070, USA

John Norris has asserted his moral right to be identified
as the author of this work.

Library of Congress Cataloging in Publication Data available

British Library Cataloguing in Publication Data
A catalogue record for this book is available from the British Library

ISBN 1 85753 177 9 Hardcover

Typeset and designed by Images Book Production Ltd
Printed by Bookcraft Ltd, Midsomer Norton, Somerset

CONTENTS

When the Allies first fielded the powerful armoured vehicles termed as tanks during the First World War, the Germans had no idea of what they were facing. Initially they were thrown into complete disarray, but with typical German thoroughness they consolidated and fought back with stoicism. The only weapons they could bring to bear on these huge lumbering machines were their field guns depressed to fire directly at the tanks. However, it was realised that this was a classic case of 'overkill', and other more economical means had to be found to destroy them.

Once it was realised that these machines were here to stay, a reliable and cost-effective method of countering them had to be found. The first dedicated anti-tank weapons to be tried were large calibre rifles, such as the 13mm, simply laid out like an over-sized bolt-action rifle weighing more than 15kg. These weapons were over 1.3m in length, which did not make them easy weapons for the infantry to handle within the confines of trench systems. Furthermore, the fierce recoil of these weapons did not make them popular. However, with a range of 70m they did allow the infantryman to engage tanks and pierce the armour plate protecting the crew. It was soon to be realised that the act of just penetrating the armour itself did not stop the tank. What such weapons needed was a chance hit striking and rupturing a fuel pipe which could start an internal fire. There was also the chance that a member of the crew could be hit.

The next phase in the anti-armour battle was the development of specialised anti-tank guns, which the Germans first developed in the form of the Rheinmetall 3.7cm gun. Weighing some 160kg, this weapon could destroy a tank in the way we know today. The British Army did not have to develop their anti-tank guns with the same urgency because the German Army only ever developed a handful of tanks, of unreliable design.

Guns continued to be the only form of anti-tank weapon used by major European armies, and these appeared in various calibres. The Second World War was to see a great change in the way in which tanks were attacked. However, all the main armies entered the conflict still equipped with anti-tank rifles – which varied in calibre by now but rarely exceeded 20mm. By and large, armies were still equipped with guns in the 3.7cm calibre, except for the British Army which had the slightly larger 2 pounder, 40mm, gun. Tanks became heavier and these weapons could not defeat their armour. The British Army took into service the 6-pounder and 17-pounder anti-tank guns which were great advances, and for their part the Germans fielded the fearsome 8.8cm gun. However, science was entering the race. The effect of hollow charge warheads was being noted and made compact enough to allow infantry to carry weapons to fire them. The British Army developed the Projector Infantry Anti-Tank, PIAT, a weapon using the spigot method of launching an anti-tank projectile. It was good at close ranges, penetrating 75mm of armour, and could be fired from within confined spaces. The Germans developed a range of disposable infantry weapons called Panzerfaust, which became increasingly more powerful as the range progressed. For example the Panzerfaust 150 could penetrate 200mm of armour, but was relatively short-ranged. The Americans developed the M1 2.36-inch anti-tank rocket launcher. This was a reusable, shoulder-fired weapon capable of penetrating 80mm of armour at 400m range. Firing an electrically initiated rocket, it was the anti-tank weapon of the war, and for some years after was the model on which other recoilless (RCL) anti-tank weapons were based.

It can be seen, therefore, that all the pieces were in place for modern anti-tank weapons to be developed and over the years that is exactly what happened. Slowly at first, but gathering pace and reputation the new generation of anti-tank weapons were invariably based around guided missile systems, because it was realised that they offered better accuracy over free-flight projectiles. Recoilless systems still remain in service around the world and in some cases conventional anti-tank guns too. These, it must be pointed out, are of considerable vintage and their reliability and effectiveness against well-armoured modern AFVs would be highly questionable. Shoulder-fired anti-tank weapons carried by infantry are more compact and accurate than ever before. Even the long range missiles have on-board computers to permit them to be locked onto the target either before or after launch. When this is combined with Thermal Imaging and Infra Red sights, the tank has nowhere to hide. The first guided anti-tank missiles were large cumbersome affairs, such as the Vigilant and Malkara, but technological advances have brought their overall size and weight down, while at the same time increasing their lethality.

Indeed, guided missiles have emerged as the preferred and most effective method of dealing with MBTs, especially at long ranges. Only their high cost prevents some of the smaller countries from acquiring such weapons which leaves them having to resort instead to RCLs. Free-flight projectiles are limited to a practical engagement range of 500m, because beyond that distance gravity begins to affect their trajectory and accuracy falls off. Even then, RCLs with their free-flight projectiles still proliferate and some are very powerful for their design. Smaller anti-tank weapons in the form of rifle grenades have a place on the battlefield, but again their value is questionable when pitted against MBTs. An infantryman would only use such devices against light AFVs and wheeled vehicles. Anti-tank mines are another way of destroying MBTs, but these are laid by specialised sapper or engineer units and have to be pre-laid in defensive belts to be certain of intercepting an armoured thrust with MBTs.

Attacked from above by helicopters mounting long-range anti-tank missiles and from below by anti-tank mines, not to mention infantry systems, it might appear that the days of the tank are numbered. But this is not the case and designers are fitting increasingly effective armour to them, including explosive reactive armour which can negate the effects of conventional hollow charge warheads. In turn the designers of anti-tank weapons are developing ever more powerful anti-tank weapons including HEAT warheads laid out in tandem. A conventional and continuous arms race between the tank designer and anti-tank designer is being conducted as first one side then the other becomes superior in design. Individual infantrymen now have the capability to strike back at one of the most powerful systems deployed on the battlefield. But today the helicopter is the deadly foe of the MBT and when carrying banks of ATGWs with ranges of 4000m and beyond, they have to be considered the ultimate in platforms for anti-tank weapons with vehicle mounted systems coming a close second. The battlefield survivability rate of an infantryman using an anti-tank system such as the M-47 Dragon and Milan is quite low, yet that has not prevented countries such as Britain from establishing what in effect are specialised anti-tank units. For example 24 Airmobile Brigade of the British Army is heavily equipped with anti-tank weapons ranging from disposable, shoulder-fired weapons to Milan and even having TOW-armed helicopters available to it. This is a forward-looking battlefield development and one that will influence tactical doctrines of the future.

This book concentrates on anti-tank weapons that are available to infantry, either directly or as support weapons – such as minefields or the new generation of anti-tank mortar rounds which attack from above. For obvious reasons it has been decided that various specialised anti-tank weapons such as the Copperhead cannon-launched anti-tank projectile, the dual-purpose ADATS, Air Defence Anti-Tank System, and the air-launched Maverick missile, should be covered separately in the relevant books in this series.

AA: Anti-Armour. Simplified expression meaning the same as anti-tank.

ACLOS: Automatic Command to Line Of Sight. This is a highly advanced for of anti-tank missile guidance system, whereby the missile's seeker head can identify its target and home in on it without the need of input from the firer. Also known as 'third generation' or 'fire and forget' guidance.

AFV: Armoured Fighting Vehicle.

AP: Armour Piercing. Identifies solid projectile for the kinetic energy attack of armour. Used from anti-tank guns and main armament of main battle tanks.

APC: Armoured Personnel Carrier.

AT: Anti-Tank.

ATGW: Anti-Tank Guided Weapon. Term used to identify guided weapons as opposed to free-flight. The firer guides the missile towards its target by means of a manual control.

Chemical energy: Explosive power is used to defeat the target rather than solid shot.

CLOS: (Sometimes referred to as COLOS) Command to Line Of Sight.

CLGP: Cannon Launched Guided Projectile. Often referred to as smart munitions, this is a round of ammunition fired from an artillery piece and contains on-board computers and sensors to locate and home in on target vehicle from above.

CM: Countermeasure; a means of defeating missile guidance usually through electronic measures.

DP: Dual-purpose. Usually high explosive warhead capable of being used against various targets, not just vehicles, such as buildings and infantry in the open.

DS: Discarding sabot. Term used with ammunition fired from the main armament of a main battle tank. Special 'petals' drop off the core when it leaves the muzzle to produce high velocity.

ECM: Electronic countermeasures. See CM.

ERA: Explosive Reactive Armour. Special box-like devices filled with explosive compound and set to detonate away from vehicle. The devices are bolted on to MBTs and are designed to explode when struck by an anti-tank projectile carrying a HEAT warhead and prematurely detonate it away from the main armour protection of the vehicle.

FFR: Free flight rocket. Projectile which has no guidance, such as RCL ammunition.

Fin stabilised: Missiles use fin stabilisation during flight to impart a slight roll for stability during time of flight to target. Projectiles fired by anti-tank guns can also be fin stabilised.

Fuse: An electronic device used in a missile capable of sensing or detecting the target. It does not usually contain explosive components and serves only to initiate the projectiles explosive payload, typically a HEAT charge.

HE: High Explosive. Denotes chemical composition of warhead filling.

HEAA: High Explosive Anti-Armour. American term for HEAT.

HEAP: High Explosive Armour Piercing. American term for HEAT.

HEAT: High Explosive Anti-Tank. Specialised warhead fitted to an anti-tank missile or other projectile, which uses shaped or hollow charge principle to defeat the target with a jet of molten metal and gas.

HEDP: High Explosive Dual Purpose. Term used to describe warhead with high explosive content and used against buildings and vehicles.

HEFT: High Explosive Follow Through. Term meaning tandem effect warhead. See Tandem.

9

HESH: High Explosive Squash Head. A base-fused warhead of an anti-tank projectile. Similar in effect to HEAT, in that it is a chemical warhead. It uses a large blast effect rather than a jet of molten gas and metal. Can also be used against buildings.

Hollow Charge: Expression used to define explosive charge, the face of which nearest the target has been pre-formed into a cone and lined with metal such as copper. When detonated by a crush fuse the explosive energy is directed by the hollow area to form a high-speed jet of molten metal and gas to penetrate the armour of a vehicle. Also known as the 'Monroe' or 'Neuman' effect. See also Shaped Charge.

HV: High Velocity. Term used for ammunition fired by anti-tank gun.

HVAP: High Velocity Armour Piercing. Term used with ammunition fired by anti-tank gun.

HVAPFSDS: High Velocity Armour Piercing Fin Stabilised Discarding Sabot. Type of ammunition used by anti-tank gun.

HVAPDS: High Velocity Armour Piercing Discarding Sabot. Type of ammunition used by anti-tank guns.

(The above four terms all refer to ammunition used from either anti-tank guns or the main armament of MBTs or self-propelled anti-tank vehicles)

IR: Infra Red. Method of night observation using the IR end of the spectrum range. It can be either passive or active to detect or 'illuminate' a target at night. Passive IR is also known as Thermal Imaging.

Kinetic energy: Usually a solid shot or long-rod penetrator of Tungsten or depleted uranium using its tensile strength and high velocity to defeat armour.

LAV: Light Armoured Vehicle.

LAW: Light Anti-Armour Weapon.

LRGW: Long range guided weapon. Same as ATGW, but specified as being long range.

MBT: Main Battle Tank.

MCLOS: Manual Command to Line of Sight. Method of guidance whereby the firer steers the missile on to its target by means of a manual control. Also referred to as 'first generation guidance'.

NATO: North Atlantic Treaty Organisation.

PGM: Precision Guided Munition. Smart munition using the light from a laser target illuminating device to home in on its target.

PIBD: Point Initiating Base Detonating. Type of fuse fitted to hollow charge, HEAT, warheads. A sensitive tip at the front of the warhead strikes the target first and initiates the detonator at the base of the charge.

RCL: Recoilless. Method of firing an anti-tank weapon without producing the recoil forces generated by normal artillery. A jet of gas or counter-mass force, usually plastic pellets, ejects from the rear of the weapon on firing to balance out the force of the projectile's discharge.

SACLOS: Semi-Automatic Command to Line of Sight. Most widely used method of anti-tank missile guidance system, whereby the firer simply gathers the target image into his optical sight and tracks it for the duration of the missile flight. An in-built computer within the missile responds to course corrections passed to it through a fine trailing wire from the firer's position.

SPATG: Self-propelled anti-tank guns. Sometimes referred to as tank destroyers.

Spin Stabilised: Artillery shells are spin stabilised for accuracy and this applies to some anti-tank projectiles. A round of ammunition usually fired from an artillery piece and containing an in-built guidance system to scan for a target in its terminal, or end of trajectory phase, of flight. That is to say, before it impacts a scanner searches for a suitable target, such as an MBT, at it homes in on it.

Thermal Imaging: See IR.

TOW: Tube-launched Optically-tracked Wire-guided. American-built anti-tank missile using SACLOS and widely used and copied.

ARGENTINA

The Model 1968 RCL in service with the Argentinian Army has a calibre of 105mm and is capable of firing both HE and HEAT rounds out to a maximum range of 9,200m. At this extreme range the accuracy of the weapon would be in question and therefore one can assume that only HE rounds would be fired out to this range for harassment effect of infantry in assembly areas. The HEAT rounds would probably not be fired at targets much beyond 1,200m, which is also the effective range of the 7.62mm spotting rifle, but the telescopic sight is calibrated for ranges out to 1,800m and is fitted with a stadiametric ladder anti-tank sight. The Model 1968 RCL can be fired from several positions. In its basic form this Argentinian weapon is towed on a two-wheeled carriage from which it can also be fired in three settings, high, medium and low. This last firing setting for the weapon has a silhouette height of only 620mm, which is good for firing on targets from concealed positions and increasing the battlefield survivability of the crew. The weapon can be mounted on a tripod for use in defensive positions. A wide range of vehicles, both tracked and wheeled, can be configured to carry the Model 1968.The weapon is served by a crew of four, who can achieve a rate of fire of around three to five rounds per minute. The cylindrical combustion chamber is perforated and the breech-block is centrally hinged for quick operation. If this mechanism becomes damaged it can easily be replaced even in combat situations, with only a minimum of delay in firing time. The firing mechanism is mechanically operated and the firing pin initiates the primer at the base of the round which in turn ignites the propellant charge. The blast to the rear of the weapon is fierce and the danger range is set at 40m spread out over a 90 degree angle. This hardly lends the Model 1968 to covert operations. This weapon is used by the Argentinian Army in following with other forces in the region who still have a use for RCL weapons of this nature. The hollow charge round can penetrate 200mm of armour and the telescopic sight is a x4 unit with a 12 degree field of view. The Model 1968 can be elevated between -7 and +40 degrees with a full 360 degree traverse on the carriage to allow the fullest movement to engage a series of targets.

Calibre:	105mm
Barrel length:	3m
Overall length:	4.020m
Height road trim:	1.070m
Weight:	397kg
Weight of spotting rifle:	6.4kg

AMMUNITION

	HE	HEAT
Weight:	15.6kg	11.1kg
Muzzle velocity:	400m/sec	400m/sec

The weapon uses the gases produced from firing the 105mm round in a very efficient manner. The chamber is oversized and provides low loading density to impart optimum use of the propellant gases. The Model 1974 is mounted on a two-wheeled carriage for towing, and from which it can also be fired. In its firing role a stabilising arm is lowered to provide a three-point firing platform. The carriage can be set to three firing heights, low, medium and high.

The body of the venturi contains a pair of spiral vanes to compensate for the torque forces between the rifling in the barrel and the shell – which can be either fin-stabilised or spin-stabilised – as it passes along the barrel. The breech-block is hinged and can be rapidly replaced in the field if it becomes damaged in combat. The Model 1974 can be elevated between -7 and +45 degrees with a full 360 degree traverse.

The weapon is aimed by means of a x4 magnification optical sight which has a 12 degree field of view and is calibrated out to 1,800m with a stadiametric ladder anti-tank sight. For additional accuracy a 7.62mm calibre heavy automatic rifle is fitted and this has a range of 1200m. This is used in the way of all other spotting rifle systems: once the operator is satisfied his aim is correct to the target he will quickly fire two or three 7.62mm rounds and observe the fall of shot. If they strike the target he will fire the main 105mm round.

The Model 1974 is served by a crew of four and can fire either HE or HEAT rounds at the rate of three to five rounds per minute. The 16.6kg HE round achieves a muzzle velocity of 400m/sec and can be fired out to 9,200m range. In effect the Model 1974 is just a more powerful upgraded Model 1968 RCL, a weapon with which it shares many common features. However, the Model 1974 fires heavier ammunition with improved firing angles. The HEAT round weighs 14.7kg and achieves a muzzle velocity of 514m/sec.

Calibre:	105mm
Barrel length:	3m
Overall length:	4.020m
Height in towing condition:	1.070m
Weight in firing mode:	397kg
Crew:	4

The Mathogo range of anti-tank missiles was developed for the Argentinian Army during the 1970s by a local company. The missiles are MCLOS guided and no doubt were influenced in design by the now obsolete Vigilant anti-tank missile of the British Army. The Mathogo is man-portable but can just as easily be adapted for launching from a carrier armoured vehicle. The Argentinians have experimented with fitting the Mathogo to helicopters, but the accuracy of the missile range in this role is not what it should be for anti-tank purposes.

The warhead of the Mathogo is the standard HEAT charge to allow 400mm of armour to be penetrated. One version of the Mathogo has a target engagement range between 400m and 2,000m, whilst the other version can engage targets between 400m and 3000m. The missile is launched from a watertight container, which is beneficial in adverse weather conditions. The operator can set his control unit to control the firing of up to four missiles which are tactically sited up to 50m distance away from his actual position.

The MCLOS guidance of the Mathogo range of missiles is typical of this missile series. After an initial boost launch, a sustainer motor engages and spoilers on the missile's fins impart course corrections during time of flight to target, which is quite slow at 90m/sec. Both the 2,000m and 3,000m range Mathogo missiles can be fired using the same control unit and optical sight, which eases operational readiness.

Length:	998mm
Body diameter:	102mm
Span:	470mm
Weight:	11.3kg
Weight of launcher:	8.2kg
Speed:	90m/sec
Range (min/max):	400m/2,000-3,000m
Penetration:	400mm

As the Argentinians based their Mathogo range of missiles on the Vigilant, so they based their Cibel-2K anti-tank missile on the older Mathogo missile. This does not imply they did not make any advances in anti-tank technology. In fact they appear to have learned a considerable number of lessons in weapon technology which are reflected in the design of the Cibel-2K.

This weapon is a second generation anti-tank missile using SACLOS guidance and was introduced in the 1980s for the Argentine Army. The Cibel guidance system uses a near-IR sensible TV area sensor to gather the missile on to the target. Apart from this it functions in much the same way as other SACLOS systems. The design is advanced and incorporates a number of in-built countermeasures.

Like the older Mathogo missile, the Cibel is launched from a pre-loaded carrying box for ease of transport. Indeed it can be remotely fired by the operator who can be sited up to 50m away from the point of launch of the weapon. In this role, up to 12 Cibel missiles can be pre-sited and controlled remotely, with the operator capable of launching two missiles per minute from a defensive position. Trials conducted recently show that Cibel is better than 90% lethal against a medium tank at 2000m range.

The firing post of the Cibel-2K weighs 12kg with the tripod. The telescopic sight unit has x20 magnification and there is also an image intensifier unit for night operations. The TI system allows the missile to be fired under all weather conditions, with a 24 hour availability.

AUSTRIA

The American-designed M40A1 recoilless anti-tank weapon is one of the most widely used weapons of its type and age still in service. It is currently still in service with the Austrian Army in two forms, but is still basically the same weapon. The first form is in the vehicle mounted role where it can be used to fire directly from a special mount to give a full 360 degree traverse. Second is the towed version of the weapon, which is mounted on a two-wheeled carriage, and is of Austrian design.

The vehicle-mounted version of the M40A1 RCL allows the crew and ammunition to be carried in one vehicle to take on battlefield tank hunting roles. The towed version of the M40A1 operates from the highly stable carriage and can be set either high or low. The first setting allows it to be used from behind cover, whilst the second, or low setting, gives a low silhouette and thereby presents a smaller target when engaging a vehicle.

It is claimed that the M40A1 has a rate of fire of five rounds per minute, but one is inclined to believe that such a rate of fire would not be used in the anti-tank role where only well-aimed shots count in destroying a vehicle. Furthermore, the claimed maximum range of 6,900m is probably the farthest distance the shell will carry beyond the target should the crew miss. Very few anti-tank weapons of this type would engage a vehicle beyond 500m, because after that range gravity begins to affect the trajectory of a free-flight shell. However, designs along these lines, indeed many versions of the M40A1 RCL, are still in use where the military budget is constrained.

Calibre:	106mm
Elevation:	-17 to +65 degrees
Traverse:	360 degrees
Weight (battle order):	113.9kg
Weight of shell:	7.71kg
Muzzle velocity:	503m/sec
Maximum range:	6,900m

The M40A2 RCL is basically a continuation of the widely used and highly popular M40 RCL series. The M40A2 is of the same calibre, 106mm, and fires HEAT and HEP-T (high explosive practice – tracer). This last type of ammunition is used for training purposes. The small army of Cameroon still holds at least 40 RCLs of the type M40A2, making it one of the last users of this type of weapon.

The weapon can be towed on a two-wheeled carriage, but is more popularly mounted on a fixing for direct firing from a 4x4 wheeled vehicle. The M40A2 fires its HEAT round at 308m per second out to a maximum range of 2,745m, but the practical anti-tank range is just over 1,000m. The weapon can traverse a full 360 degrees and elevate between -17 degrees and +65 degrees and realistically achieve the rate of fire of one round per minute. It is crewed by two to four men and features the standard 12.7mm spotting rifle to aid ranging onto targets. It weighs 220kg in its travelling mode, which makes it light enough to be manhandled over rough terrain if necessary.

Calibre:	106mm
Barrel length:	2.840m
Length overall:	3.4m
Range maximum:	2745m (HEAT)
Crew:	2-4
Weight:	220kg
Muzzle velocity:	308m/sec

BELGIUM

Although designed primarily for anti-tank purposes, this light gun of the Belgian Army in 90mm calibre can be used fire various types of ammunition, including smoke for screening movement of friendly infantry and vehicles. It can also fire fragmentation rounds for engaging enemy infantry and light vehicles in the open. In this latter role the 5.21kg round has a lethal radius of 50m and can be fired out to a range of 4,200m to assist in breaking up the formations of enemy forces as they advance.

In its anti-tank role the 90mm Light Gun fires a HEAT round weighing 3.54kg, of which 2.28kg constitutes the actual projectile, at a muzzle velocity of 338m/sec. The HEAT round will travel out to 3,500m but the effective combat engagement range is in the region of 1,000m. The HEAT round is 635mm in length and can be used in a dual role. It will penetrate 1,200mm of concrete to destroy fixed positions, and is capable of penetrating 350mm of armour. There is also a 5.95kg canister round containing over 1,100 steel pellets for anti-personnel roles. This can engage targets out to 300m, which could include soft-skinned vehicles.

There are two versions of the 90mm Light Gun: the CAN-90H which is 416kg in weight, and the CAN-90L which weighs 285kg. Both versions can fire all natures of ammunition available in the 90mm range.

Calibre:	90mm
Weight:	CAN-90L, 285kg
	CAN-90H, 416kg
Overall height:	CAN-90L, 350mm
	CAN-90H, 400mm
Overall width:	CAN-90L, 290mm
	CAN-90H, 450mm
Barrel length:	2.9m (both versions)
Muzzle velocity:	633m/sec
Range:	3500m maximum. 1000m effective
Arming distance:	16m
Pentration:	350mm (armour) 1200mm (concrete)

The shoulder-fired RL-83 'Blindicide' anti-tank rocket launcher was developed in Belgium in two versions, the standard version and the long-range rocket version. It is now declared obsolete with the Belgian Army, but may still be used by some client states, especially those in Africa. The RL-83 is of 83mm calibre and is mechanically-fired and operated by a crew of two men. The weapon incorporates three sighting methods. There are either open or optical sights with allowances for angular correction for use out to ranges of 400m. The third type is an auxiliary sight to allow target engagement out to 900m.

The weapon is collapsible, and in its collapsed state it is only 920mm in length. The long range ammunition is of HEAT type and is 570mm in length and weighs 2.4kg with a maximum velocity of 300m/sec in flight. It has a practical range of 500m and will penetrate either 300mm or armour or one metre of concrete. The standard RL-83 fires either HEAT rounds or HE anti-personnel, with the capability of also firing illuminating, smoke or incendiary rounds.

Calibre:	83mm
Crew:	2
Length:	920mm folded, 1,700mm extended
Weight:	8.4kg
Range:	400m to 900m
Muzzle velocity:	100m/sec with standard round

The RLC-83 is a compact development of the Belgian-designed RL-83 Blindicide. In many respects the weapons are identical, with the overall length being the distiguishing factor. In this case the RLC-83 is 1,200mm in extended length compared to the 1,700mm of the RL-83, with a weight reduction of nearly 25%. The operational sequences are the same but intended to use only the long-range ammunition.

It is crewed by two men who can achieve a rate of fire of up to ten rounds per minute if necessary. The sight unit is a simplified optical device and the firing mechanism remains mechanical. The specifications of the rounds are the same as the long-range type used with the BL-83 (qv) and are of the HEAT type. Like the RL-83, this anti-tank weapon is also classed as obsolete with the Belgian Army, having been replaced with the likes of Milan, but is still likely to be found in use with client states, especially those in the sub-Saharan region.

Calibre:	83mm
Overall length:	1,200mm
Weight:	6.2kg
Crew:	2
Launch velocity:	120m/sec
Penetration:	300mm armour, 1m concrete

BRAZIL

This is an elderly design RCL anti-tank weapon, even for the Brazilian Army, but one which still works well nevertheless. In fact it is a direct copy of the American-designed M18A1, also of 57mm calibre, but was declared obsolete a number of years ago with the American Army. Brazil has for some reason identified a requirement for such a weapon which no doubt makes sense to them. It can only be assumed that the terrain in central and southern America being unsuited to large-scale attack by heavily armoured vehicles has led the Brazilian Army to concentrate on anti-tank weapons which can engage APCs and other light vehicles, whilst leaving those heavier armoured vehicles which might venture on to the battlefield to other weapons systems such as artillery. The Brazilian Army's M18A1 RCL can be fired from a pintel mounting on a light 4X4 wheel drive vehicle over a limited broadside arc, or in extreme cases, dismounted and operated as a two-man shoulder-fired weapon. This particular version built under licence in Brazil is claimed to have a barrel life of 2500 rounds and the breech block and throat will last for 500 firings. This type of weapon, and all other similar types of RCLs of a comparable calibre, have a useful application with guerrilla forces, who find its operation simple to use in ambush situations against the vehicles of Government forces. The M18A1 is a percussion fired weapon, which has a maximum range of nearly 4000m and is capable of firing HE and HEAT rounds. Light wheeled vehicles and some older designed APCs could suffer damage if engaged by this weapon but heavier armoured vehicles are unlikely to be affected by the light rounds.

Calibre:	57mm
Crew:	Two men
Overall weight:	25kg
Overall length:	1.564m
Muzzle velocity:	365m/sec
Range:	450m effective

CHINA

The Type 51 RCL anti-tank weapon is a Chinese copy of the American-designed M-20 3.5 inch (89mm) rocket launcher. Although officially declared obsolete, the Type 51 is still to be found in service with several countries in the Far East. For all practical purposes the Type 51 has the same characteristics as the M-20 (qv) and can be dismantled into two parts for ease of carrying by infantrymen in the same manner. It is served by two men, who act as firer and loader.

The Type 51 fires electrically initiated HEAT projectiles. Rather bulky in its firing role, the Type 51 can be carried in its collapsed state by infantrymen operating from APCs, who would then assemble it for firing after deploying from the APC. This procedure would allow spare ammunition to be carried by members of the combat section/squad operating from the same vehicle.

Calibre:	90mm
Overall length:	1530mm assembled ready for firing
Length dismantled:	762mm
Overall weight:	5.45kg
Range:	1200m
Armour penetration:	267mm
Muzzle velocity:	98.6m/sec
Crew:	2

The Type 52 RCL is nothing more than a Chinese copy of the obsolete M-20 RCL of American design. In fact, so closely is it based on the original design that it can be used to fire ammunition of either American or Chinese manufacture. Although declared obsolete by China itself, some sources claim this weapon still in current service with the Chinese Army. If that is the case it is probably in reserve war stock, due to its limited capability of defeating armour, being set at only 228mm.

The Type 52 RCL, like the larger Type 51 RCL, is of 75mm calibre. It has a perforated, hinged breech block and can fire either HE or HEAT ammunition, the former having a maximum range of 6675m for engaging soft targets. This weapon can be towed behind a variety of vehicles on its light two-wheeled carriage and is served by a crew of two or three. For firing, the wheels of the carriage are usually removed and deployed as a tripod for greater stability. The overall light weight of the Type 52 allows it to be manhandled into prepared positions for defensive actions if necessary and it has an effective anti-tank range of some 800m. Should it be issued for combat the Type 52 RCL would probably be used against APCs.

Calibre:	75mm
Weight:	85.1kg
Overall length:	2.132m
Max range HE:	6675m
Armour penetration:	228mm
Crew:	2-3

Sources disagree over the current status of the Chinese Type 56 anti-tank grenade launcher of 80mm calibre. Some declare it to be totally obsolete while others refer to it as still being in frontline service. It would, therefore, perhaps be more fair to state that if the Type 56 is still in service its capability would be of highly doubtful usefulness in combat and is likely to be used by reserve troops.

The Type 56 is nothing more than a copy of the Russian RPG-2. It is a reusable shoulder-fired anti-tank grenade launcher and is capable of firing either Type 50 HEAT ammunition of Chinese manufacture or Russian manufactured ammunition. The Chinese ammunition is believed to be the more powerful of the two types and is thought to be capable of penetrating some 265mm of armour compared to the Russian ammunition of the same calibre which will only penetrate between 150mm and 175mm of armour.

The Type 56 may be held in large numbers in war stock, but with instructions to be used only against softer targets such as light wheeled vehicles. The weapon is loaded and operated in the same manner as the more familiar RPG-7 and Type 69 launchers.

Calibre of warhead:	80mm
Calibre of launcher:	40mm
Overall length of launcher:	1.194m
Weight unloaded:	2.83kg
Maximum effective range:	150m
Weight of projectile:	1.84kg
Rate of fire:	4-6rpm

The Type 65 RCL is yet another Chinese copy of a Russian-designed anti-tank weapon. This time it is based on the B-10 recoilless gun, and whilst it has been declared obsolete that is no reason to believe it is no longer in service anywhere, because such weapons are favoured by guerrilla forces.

The overall performance of the Type 65 matches that of the Russian B-10, and is fitted with a multi-vented breech-block with an enlarged chamber section for recoilless operation. The Type 65 can fire HE, high explosive, and HEAT (high explosive anti-tank) ammunition to engage both vehicles and fixed points such as forward artillery positions.

It is a towed weapon, having a light two-wheeled carriage, but is usually mounted on a tripod for firing to give a full 360 degree traverse. Its low weight allows crew to manhandle the Type 65 over rough terrain and obstacles for siting in positions to overlook strategic routes for ambush.

The HE round weighs 4.5kg and can be fired out to a maximum range of 4,470m. Of limited ability, the Type 65 is still quite capable of defeating APCs and similar vehicles.

Calibre:	82mm
Barrel length:	1,659mm
Overall length:	1,677mm
Travelling weight:	87.6kg
Weight of HEAT round:	3.6kg
Muzzle velocity:	320m/sec
Maximum effective range:	390m in anti-tank role
Armour penetration:	240mm

On first glance at the Chinese Type 69 anti-tank weapon one is left in no doubt as to its origins, and cross-referencing only serves to confirm that it is indeed a copy of the famous Russian RPG-7 anti-tank grenade launcher. The Type 69 is shoulder-fired and has a maximum range of 500m against a static target. Should the firer miss the grenade will continue in flight and self-destruct at 920m range. This is probably intended as a safety action to reduce the hazard of unexploded rounds to the user's own side as it advances.

Introduced into service in 1972, the Type 69 is a reusable weapon which has all the same characteristics and overall performance of the RPG-7. It is still in widespread use, being popular with guerrilla and terrorist groups. Several countries, including Iraq and India, manufacture their own copy of the RPG-7.

Calibre of launcher:	40mm
Calibre of projectile:	85mm
Overall length of launcher:	990mm
Weight of launcher:	7kg
Weight of projectile:	2.25kg
Muzzle velocity:	300m/sec
Range static target:	500m
Range moving target:	300m
Penetration of armour:	320mm at zero obliquity

CZECHOSLOVAKIA

M59 AND M59A RCL 33

Two versions of the Czech M59 RCL exist: the original M59 which has a smooth finish to its exterior surfaces and the M59A which has a finned exterior to the chamber to assist in cooling. In practice the rate of fire would not be so high as to create such a problem, but someone thought such a move was necessary and so the M59A version of the weapon was developed. Apart from that small point both types of RCL are identical and function in the same manner.

Both weapons are in service with the Czech army and can be towed on a robust two-wheeled carriage behind a wide range of vehicles. The M59 range of RCLs can also be mounted on top of APCs for use in the anti-tank role – in a manner similar to the old Wombat RCL of the British Army with the FV432 APC. The light weight of the M59 allows it to be manhandled over rough terrain if necessary, for which purpose a special harness is attached to a 'T-bar' on the muzzle of the weapon.

The M59 weapons can fire HEAT and HE rounds. In addition to the optical sight a ranging/spotting rifle is also fitted. The ammunition types both weigh 6kg and the HE round can be fired out to a range of over 6,650m, but the effective range of the HEAT round is set at 1,200m. The M59 is served by a crew of five and is now limited in its ability to destroy MBTs, especially those types fitted with ERA. Therefore the M59 would best be employed against APCs and infantry in the open with HE rounds. The weapon has a full 360 degree traverse at zero degrees elevation, which is reduced to 60 degrees of traverse when it is elevated to an angle of 25 degrees to increase range.

Calibre:	82mm
Crew:	5
Overall length:	4,597mm
Width:	1,675mm
Height:	1,000mm
Elevation:	-13 degrees to +25 degrees
Weight:	385kg
Maximum effective range (HEAT):	1,220m
Muzzle velocity:	745m/sec with HEAT
Penetration:	250mm

FINLAND

The M-55 is the current light anti-tank weapon equipping the infantry of the Finnish Army. A reloadable, shoulder-fired infantry weapon, the M-55 is of a better design than other weapons of comparable ability. The M-55 is 55mm in calibre and like the Russian RPG series of anti-tank grenade launchers shares the somewhat unusual method of loading the projectile into the front of the launcher. It is aimed by means of simple sights clipped to the launching tube. This reusable weapon was developed locally in Finland and is at present issued at the rate of six launchers per company in a motorised battalion.

Calibre:	55mm
Length of launcher:	940mm
Length with round loaded:	1,240mm
Weight of weapon:	8.5kg
Weight of projectile:	2.5kg
Effective anti-tank range:	200m
Rate of fire:	3-5rpm
Armour penetration:	200mm

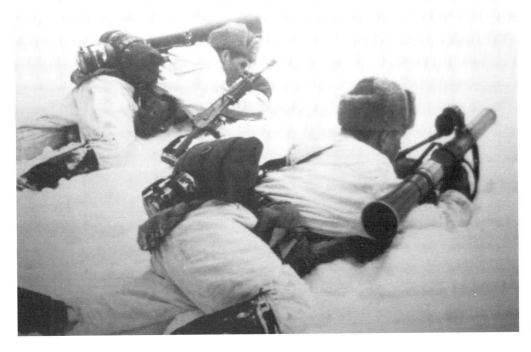

The reliance of the Finnish Army on free-flight anti-tank projectiles is once more illustrated by the 95 SM58-61 recoilless gun of 95mm calibre. This is a crew-served weapon, requiring three men to operate it. It is mounted on a two-wheeled carriage on which it is towed and from which it can be fired.

The 95 SM58-61 weighs only 40kg in its combat order and carrying handles located at four points allow it to be manhandled over rough terrain for siting in defensive positions. It is comparable in performance to the now obsolete Wombat of the British Army and can fire either HE or HEAT shells. The HE shell weighs 12.7kg and can be used to engage targets out to 2,000m. The HEAT shell weighs 10.2kg of which 4.6kg is the actual projectile. This round is capable of penetrating 300mm of armour out to ranges of 1,000m. The weapon is stated as being capable of firing between six and eight rounds per minute. Presumably this is the HE round fired against a static target, because tracking to engage a moving target would not allow such a rate of fire.

The SM58-61 is currently in service with the heavy weapons companies of Finnish Army infantry battalions. The Finnish Army is stated as being the only force using this weapon. Even for its age the SM58-61 is still a useful weapon and its light weight allows it to be manhandled by its crew into prepared defensive positions.

Calibre:	95mm
Crew:	3
Barrel length:	3.2m
Weight in combat role:	140kg
Muzzle velocity:	615m/sec (HEAT)
Effective range:	1,000m (HEAT)

FRANCE

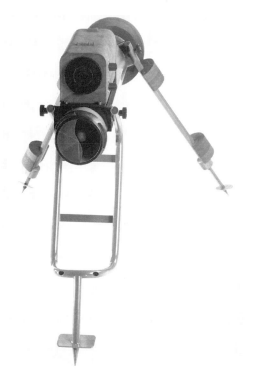

who have a global commitment, ranging from arctic conditions to desert warfare.

Apilas has one other application in that it can be deployed as a 'stand alone' device to engage AFVs. Mounted on a special cradle, Apilas can be configured to serve as an off-route anti-tank weapon to engage vehicles from the side as they pass. In this particular role it is purely defensive and only sited along those routes likely to be used by enemy forces. It can be configured to be command fired by an operator, or to be fired automatically by means of sensors mounted on the cradle. In this stand-alone role the usefulness of the Apilas is multiplied without degrading its overall performance.

Apilas is not a counter-mass recoilless weapon and must therefore be fired from a site which is clear behind.

Specifications, Infantry shoulder-fired role:

Total weight:	9kg
Overall length:	1.26m
Calibre of projectile:	112mm
Effective range:	500 to 600m
Muzzle velocity:	293m/sec

The French Army's anti-tank weapon, known as the Apilas, was designed specifically to allow the standard infantryman to engage and destroy armoured fighting vehicles. Apilas is in service with the French Army and several overseas forces. Weighing some 9kg, the Apilas is rather heavy for an infantryman to carry along with his normal complement of combat equipment. However it fires a projectile of 112mm calibre, which contains 1.5kg of explosive in a shaped charge warhead, allowing it to be used against armoured vehicles out to ranges in excess of 500m, and destroy them.

The actual projectile, which is pre-loaded into the firing tube, weighs 4.3kg and can defeat better than 720mm of steel armour plate. This shoulder-fired, disposable weapon has 'pop out' sights mounted to allow the infantryman to quickly engage a target without having to clip on the sights. Accuracy of the Apilas is such that a well-trained operator will obtain a strike within 250mm of the point of aim at 300m range, which is very good for a free-flight rocket and gives a good chance of first round hit. It can be operated in temperatures between -31C to +51C, which makes it useful for rapid deployment forces

The DARD 120 is another anti-tank weapon which been specially developed to equip French Army infantrymen with a weapon for use at section (fighting group/squad) strength. It can be carried by infantry deploying from helicopters, APCs or assault craft. The large 120mm calibre projectile, combined with high launch speed, which is sustained throughout its flight, makes the DARD accurate to all ranges.

Calibre:	120mm
Weight:	Pre-loaded launch tube
	10kg, firing mechanism 4.5kg
Overall length ready for firing:	1.96m
Maximum effective range:	600m
Muzzle velocity:	280m/sec

It is a shoulder-fired recoilless type weapon and has very little in the way of frontal signature. The backblast area effect is also reduced when fired. The DARD 120 is intended for use at relatively short ranges, with 600m being the optimum operating range. It is based on the splitting breech-block system, which is both simple and quick to use. The weapon comprises of a reusable firing device and the pre-loaded munition tube which clips on, and is discarded after firing. The actual connection between the firing device and launch tube is made by a simple quick release system.

The reusable firing device, which houses the firing mechanism and optical sights, weighs only 4.5kg and is 0.76m in length. The pre-loaded launch tube with the projectile weighs 10kg and is 1.20m in length. With operating ranges between -31 C and + 51 C the DARD is ideal for use by Rapid Deployment Forces in terrain ranging from arctic conditions to desert conditions.

The warhead of the DARD projectile is HEAT and weighs 3.3kg of which 1.9kg is the explosive charge. Time of flight to 340m is 1.2 seconds, with a flight time of 2.1 seconds out to 600m. The projectile can be used against concrete or armoured vehicles, to allow an infantryman flexibility over target engagement. In the first instance it will penetrate 2.25m and against vehicles it has been shown to be capable of defeating 850mm of homogeneous steel.

DARD can be fitted with a night vision sight to allow operating ranges between 150m and 400m. Troops carrying the components of the DARD 120 can operate in complete safety from helicopters and APCs without undue hindrance.

The Eryx is a French-designed and built anti-tank missile system which has only been in mass production since 1991, but already equips the French Army and is beginning to enter service with the Norwegian and Canadian armies.

Known commonly as the Eryx, this is a short-range anti-tank missile intended for use by dismounted infantry units to engage armoured vehicles with direct fire. It is compact enough to be carried and operated by one man and can be issued to troops down to infantry sections. It is also small enough to be carried by airborne forces and other special forces units such as marines, in addition to their other specialised equipment. The Eryx can be used to engage main battle tanks in head-on situations and can just as easily be used to engage machine gun emplacements and other defended points.

The weapon has been called the 'mini Milan', after the system which it so closely resembles. It comprises a pre-loaded firing tube and launching post which weigh 12kg and 5kg respectively. The Eryx has an initial low speed launch sequence that allows it to be fired from within confined spaces, including buildings. Capable of being shoulder-fired in the standing position or from a launching post in a prone position, Eryx can be used to engage various targets between ranges of 50m and 600m.

The Eryx missile is fitted with SACLOS guidance and has been proven to have a high first round hit capability, even against moving targets. The warhead of Eryx has been fully optimised to make it lethal against the current range of MBTs and should still be capable of defeating those designs likely to be entering service by the end of the century.

The sight unit is a 3x magnification device and can be used in low light levels. Because of its versatility and safety in use, Eryx can be used by troops operating from APCs, helicopters, or in the specialised airborne or amphibious roles.

Length of round:	925mm
Diameter of round:	160mm
Weight of round/launcher tube:	12kg
Weight of firing post:	5kg
Range:	50m to 600m
Maximum terminal speed:	245m/sec
Armour penetration:	900mm of uniform steel

The Franco-German 'Haut subsonique Optiquement Teleguide', HOT anti-tank guided weapon, is a real heavyweight missile which tips the scales at 32kg, and has an impressive overall performance. The missile itself weighs 23kg, but coming in a pre-loaded launch tube allows it to be handled in safety as a complete round of ammunition. This is a common feature to most anti-tank weapons, including the smaller ones. The heavy weight of a HOT missile complete in a launcher tube means it usually has to be mounted on a platform for firing, and except for the French Army's ATL single round launcher, the HOT is carried in multiple round launchers.

HOT is currently used by 16 countries in one form or another, including France and Germany, the two countries that developed the system originally. It is a highly versatile weapon system capable of being mounted in a variety of helicopters and fitting a wide range of AFVs as carrier vehicles. For example, the French-designed UTM800 turret will allow four HOT missiles to be mounted in a fully traversing 360 degree mount for firing from AFVs in the 5 to 12 tonne class, either tracked or wheeled, and even fixed installations.

Two HOT launch tubes are mounted either side of a central optical assembly with the UTM800 turret and this houses all the electronics for engaging a target and tracking the missile on to it. For night operations an IR system known as CASTOR is also fitted to the turret. The operator controls the turret in elevation and traverse by means of a control stick and ensures response to all commands. The UTM800 turret is fully stabilised throughout the missile launch sequence and target engagement time to maximise accuracy.

The HOT launch tubes of the UTM800 turret have to be re-loaded manually, and while this only takes a few minutes under the right conditions, it does expose a crew member to hostile fire. In the French Army the Panhard M3B vehicle can carry up to 14 HOT missiles, comprising four ready to fire from the rails of the UTM800 turret and ten reload missiles inside the vehicle. The HOT missile in its vehicle mounted role can be used to engage MBTs from 75m out to 4,000m, while from a helicopter HOT can engage targets out to a maximum range of 4,300m. This extra range over the ground-launched version is possible due to the elevated firing position of the missile.

The Lancelot is another HOT missile turret which

holds four missiles ready to fire and is a system that can be adapted to use from a wide range of AFVs. This is a two-man turret, gunner/operator and commander, which also carries a 7.62mm machine gun for engaging soft targets and self-defence. The Lancelot turret has a full 360 degree traverse and periscopic vision blocks to provide a panoramic view of the battlefield to permit the commander and gunner to engage targets quickly and simplify missile tracking. For night operations a full IR optronics range is carried. Unfortunately the Lancelot is another system that has to be reloaded outside the vehicle and exposes a crew member to the same dangers as the UTM800 turret.

The Mephisto turret on the other hand is a fully retractable launch platform for the HOT. When the platform is lowered, a crew member can reload the four launch rails from within the safety of the vehicle. In the French Army the Mephisto is fitted to VAB range of wheeled AFVs. However, it can just as easily be fitted to any other AFV in the 5 to 12 tonne class. When the platform is retracted the vehicle is indistinguishable from ordinary APCs, but when elevated to its firing position the Mephisto turret has a full 360 degree traverse and can engage targets out to 4,000m.

Like the UTM800 turret, the Mephisto is fully stabilised and carries a full complement of optical and electronic systems for the aiming, firing and controlling of HOT during target engagement.

The ATL firing post is another French development, but allows a single HOT missile to be fired from a light vehicle, either armoured or soft-skinned. Known as the Atlas mount, it has been trialled by the French Army using the light M-11 wheeled AFV as a carrier vehicle and can also be mounted either 4x4 or 6x6 jeep-type vehicles. In this mode the HOT can be used to arm light vehicles that can be deployed with airborne forces for rapid reaction duties.

The ATL also has a tripod mount for emplacing HOT as a free-standing launcher when tactical conditions dictate. In this role the capabilities of HOT are not hindered and all targets can still be engaged within the operating ranges of the missile. The ATL post weighs 410kg, with four missiles, when fitted to a vehicle, and 147kg when deployed on a tripod mounted launcher as a stand-alone system away from the carrier vehicle.

In the German Army HOT can be carried on the specialised anti-tank vehicle, the Jagdpanzer Kanone/Rakete tank destroyer. Originally these vehicles were designed to carry the SS11 anti-tank missile, but upgrading has allowed them to carry the HOT system instead, which has a number of advantages over the older system. Termed as RJPz (HOT) Jaguar 1, there

are at present some 258 of these vehicles in service with the German Army. The Jaguar 1 has a single HOT launcher mounted on the roof of the vehicle, with the operator's sight unit mounted alongside. In addition to the missile in the ready to use firing position, the Jaguar 1 can carry up to twenty reload HOT missiles internally.

HOT can be carried and fired from all helicopters with an anti-tank capability. Indeed the French Army uses it from the Gazelle and Dauphin helicopters, and the German Army uses HOT from the BO105 and BK117 helicopters. Most helicopters would carry four HOT missiles ready to fire, but the French Dauphin can carry eight missiles in two quadruple pods, one mounted either side of the fuselage.

HOT is SACLOS guided and with the helicopter-launched version a special sight, the Viviane, can be used from the French Army's Gazelle helicopter. This device is mounted in the roof of the cockpit and comprises a high-performance day sight and a passive thermal image camera for night operations. As with other missiles of this age, HOT has undergone mid-life upgrades to allow it to defeat current armour trends, including reactive armour. In fact, HOT stated as being capable of defeating all MBT types currently in service and those types likely to enter service in the foreseeable future.

Diameter of missile:	175mm
Length of missile:	1.3m
Weight of missile:	23kg
Weight of launch tube complete:	32kg
Velocity:	250m/sec
Range from vehicle:	75m to 4,000m
Range from helicopter:	4,300m (maximum)

The Individual Anti-Bunker Anti-Armour Weapon, ABB, is a dual-purpose munition which weighs 7.3kg but has a limited backblast area which makes it suitable for use during fighting in built-up areas. At present it is undergoing qualification tests with the French Army, but already it has been shown to be capable of creating a hole 250mm in diameter through a concrete wall of 200mm thickness, and penetrating 400mm of steel armour plating. The shaped charge warhead and counter-mass principle of the ABB allows members of an infantry section to engage targets out to 300m from behind defensive cover and defeat either AFVs or machine gun emplacements.

The ABB is a no-maintenance weapon which is treated as a complete round of ammunition, because of it being pre-loaded. After firing the expended device is discarded, like other similar disposable shoulder-fired anti-tank weapons. Dual-purpose weapons of this type are gaining popularity as they give the infantryman a flexible weapon to employ against a wide range of targets. The US Army, for example, has the SMAW (qv) which has been developed for similar battlefield applications.

Total weight:	7.3 kg
Overall length:	1m
Effective range:	300m
Muzzle velocity:	270m\sec

The SS11 and SS12 guided missiles were both developed in France. They can be used in the same manner as the German-developed Cobra and Mamba missiles, to which they are not dissimilar in appearance.

The SS12 is really a larger and more powerful version of the earlier developed SS11 system. Both missiles can be platform mounted on either helicopters or vehicles and are guided by means of SACLOS. They both use solid propellant rockets for their booster, have sustainer motors, and carry HEAT warheads.

These missiles are no longer in widespread use, and Argentina is one of the last users of this type of missiles. However, that is not to say they no longer have a place on the battlefield. The SS11 can be fitted with two different types of warhead to allow the flexible engagement of different types of targets. The basic HEAT warhead will defeat 600mm of armour and the special semi-perforating anti-personnel warhead will penetrate some 10mm of steel and detonate two metres beyond point of entry.

This has applications against soft targets and infantry. During the Falklands War in 1982 a British Wasp helicopter engaged the Argentinian submarine Santa Fe with SS11 missiles and severely damaged it to the point where it was forced to withdraw and no longer posed a threat to British forces. An unconventional mode of employing an anti-tank missile perhaps, but necessity is the mother of invention. The pilot saw a target of opportunity and succeeded in scoring a hit.

Iraq is known still to have a supply of SS11 missiles in war stock.

The SS12 is considerably larger than the SS11, with improved maximum engagement ranges, but apart from this is similar in layout and function. It is capable of carrying AP-FRAG warheads.

The French Army used to mount their SS11 missiles over the 75mm main armament of the AMX13 light tank on special quadruple launcher rails. This multiplied the anti-tank capabilities of the AMX13 light tank. In the German Army the Jagdpanzer Raket tank destroyer used to carry two SS11 missiles on a roof-mounted twin rail launcher with 14 reload missiles. The French Army has replaced these missile systems with the flexible Milan and HOT systems, whilst the German Army has replaced its SS11 missiles mounted on the Jagdpanzer Rakete with the HOT missile.

	SS11	SS12
Weight:	29.9kg	75kg
Length:	1.21m	1.87m
Span:	500mm	650mm
Body diameter:	164mm	180mm
Warhead:	HEAT/AP-FRAG	HEAT/AP-FRAG
Range min/max:	500m/3,000m	400m/6,000m
Speed:	685km/h	190m/sec
Guidance:	SACLOS	SACLOS

The Lance-Roquettes Anti-Char, ACL89, was developed in France to provide lightweight rocket launchers to all infantrymen who require the additional firepower to engage vehicles and infantry. The weapon has been designed to be used as either a personal weapon for anti-tank roles, or used en masse to assist in breaking up an armoured attack.

The ACL89 has two optimum engagement ranges. Firstly, at ranges up to 500 metres it can be used to engage and defeat AFVs of all types and defended positions such as machine gun emplacements. Secondly, for ranges out to 1,000m it can be used against motorised formations and the infantry acting in support. The weapon can also be carried by parachutists and marines who deploy on more specialised roles. Indeed, the ACL89 was developed with special forces, such as Rapid Deployment Forces, seen as the primary users.

The ACL89 rocket launcher comprises of a lightweight launch tube, which is inherently strong, and is collapsible in design for ease of carrying. It is shoulder-fired and can be loaded with either anti-personnel or anti-tank projectiles. In the anti-personnel role the projectile contains 1,600 steel balls of 4mm diameter, and when fired out to 800m range will produce a lethal dispersion of 25m radius. The ACL89 has a practical vehicle engagement range between 300m for moving targets and 500m for static targets. With the HEAT projectile the ACL89 is capable of defeating 500mm of steel. This makes it capable of dealing with main battle tanks, but only those types not fitted with explosive reactive armour or composite armour.

The LRAC 89mm has been in service with the French Army for some time and used in combat situations. For example when French Paras deployed to Kolwezi in Zaire to rescue European nationals caught up in the civil war in 1978, they carried LRAC 89mm weapons. On at least two occasions they were used to effectively break up attacks and are credited with being used to destroy two Russian-built light tanks and a number of other vehicles on this mission.

Calibre:	88.9mm
Length in carrying mode:	1,168mm
Length in firing mode:	1,600mm
Weight in carrying mode:	5.4kg
Weight in firing mode:	9.050kg
Muzzle velocity:	291m/sec

Technically speaking the French PIAF, Piege A Fibre Optique, Optic Fibre Trap, is not an anti-tank weapon in its own right but an add-on system for remote firing. However, the significance of such a system should not be overlooked, because it releases infantrymen to serve in their primary, more mobile, battlefield role while having a defensive system deployed for anti-tank purposes.

The PIAF is an autonomous area weapon for siting around defensive positions and can engage tanks or lighter AFVs. The system comprises of the PIAF with its integrated pressure and acoustic sensors mounted with an anti-tank weapon such as the ACL89. The PIAF device is simply mounted on the front of the French army's ACL89 canister and its electrical primer can initiate a wide range of munitions, sensing targets out to ranges of 40m, which is quite accurate for a remote sensor activated device.

When deployed on the firing tripod the device can be set up along paths, roads or concealed in doorways facing on to roads. In fact the PIAF will lend itself to applications of every type of rocket that can be remotely fired. This includes anti-personnel and anti-tank systems where it can be programmed to pick up wheeled or tracked vehicles and even infantrymen on foot patrol with its acoustic and pressure sensors respectively. It weighs only 800g and can be installed in minutes and used in temperatures ranging from -31 degrees to +60 degrees.

The French-designed WASP multi-purpose weapon is a shoulder-fired disposable weapon using the counter-mass principle to achieve recoilless operation. Capable of being carried by an infantryman, it can be used to engage either armoured fighting vehicles out to ranges of 400m or troop emplacements at a comparable range.

The WASP is a use once and throw away design which comes pre-loaded and is therefore treated as a complete round. Its counter-mass operation sequence allows it to be used from within confined spaces and is, therefore, ideal for use during fighting in built-up areas. It is capable of defeating 400mm of armour or penetrating a concrete wall of one metre thickness at a 70 degree incidence, which makes it a powerful weapon for its size.

WASP is suitable for engaging armoured personnel carriers and permits infantrymen to destroy heavy machine gun sites. A clip on night sight is available for night operations. The complete weapon weighs 3kg, of which the actual projectile weighs 550g. The low weight and compact dimensions of WASP allow three or four launchers to be carried by a single infantryman. When a full section/squad of between eight and ten men are operating from an APC, with each man carrying at least two WASP launchers, their striking power is multiplied greatly.

Overall length:	800mm
Total weight:	3kg
Calibre of projectile:	58mm
Effective range:	400m
Muzzle velocity:	250m/sec

GERMANY

The German Armbrust was originally developed as a private venture weapon for possible use with the German Army. The developing company used its own funding to develop the weapon for which there was no firm contract. Despite that, the firing trials showed the Armbrust (meaning Crossbow), to be a highly reliable and accurate weapon, which had the added capability of being fired from within confined spaces such as houses. As a result of these successful trials the benefits of the Armbrust system were realised and it was taken into service with the then West German Army.

The Armbrust is a shoulder-fired, disposable weapon which derives its recoilless effect by means of ejecting a cloud of some 5,000 plastic pellets to the rear of the operator. The signature on firing is no louder than a pistol shot and internal pistons are forced rearwards and forwards to seal the tube after firing, thereby limiting the emission of smoke and flash. In fact, the Armbrust can be fired as close as 800mm to a vertical surface to the rear, but personnel are advised not to stand in the path of the resultant plastic pellets on firing. The operator can fire Armbrust from well-concealed positions such as a slit trench and offer little in the way of profile when he fires. The light weight of the weapon – only 6.3kg, combined with its length of 850mm – means that a single infantryman can carry up to four rounds comfortably. Being a disposable weapon the launcher does not encumber the firer after use.

For normal battlefield deployment the Armbrust launcher has a simple reflex sight for target engagement. However, for special use – where a first round hit is essential, and for night operations – a clip-on, reusable laser sight can be used with the weapon. The Armbrust can be issued to troops in its pre-loaded form with either a 0.99kg HEAT projectile or a HE-fragmentation projectile, to engage armoured vehicles or infantry in the open at ranges of 330m and 1,500m respectively. The Armbrust is still in current service with the German Army, even following the re-unification of the country in 1990. It is also known to have been trialled by the US Army's 'Delta Force' special forces unit.

Calibre:	78mm
Overall length:	850mm
Complete weight:	6.3kg
Range:	330m anti-tank
Range maximum:	1500m
Armour penetration:	300mm
Muzzle velocity:	220m/sec

Argentina is among the last of the armies in the world to still find a use for these ageing anti-tank missiles. Not dissimilar in appearance to one another, the Cobra and Mamba missiles, which were both designed in West Germany, have fairly close specifications and capabilities.

The Cobra is the older of the two missile systems, originally being introduced into service with the then West German Army in 1960. It was a first generation MCLOS guided anti-tank missile operated by a single infantryman. It does not require a special launching rail from which to be fired, unlike many other systems of this type. A carrying handle is incorporated into the missile's body for ease of handling. The infantryman simply sites the Cobra missile directly on the ground in a convenient clearing, connects the command cable to the control box and the missile is ready to launch.

The warhead is HEAT and contains 2.7kg of HE. Cobra has four stabilising fins laid out in cruciform pattern with spoilers on them for control. With a range of 2,000m and capable of penetrating 500mm of armour, it was only the out-dated guidance system that led to Cobra being replaced in service by modern SACLOS guided missiles.

The Mamba missile was introduced as the replacement for the Cobra; indeed so closely do they resemble one another that the same control unit can be used to fire and guide both types of missile. The Mamba has a maximum combat range of 2,000m, and can defeat 475mm of armour with a HEAT warhead weighing 2.7kg. This is roughly comparable to the Cobra's capabilities. Four fins laid out in cruciform pattern impart fin stabilised flight to the missile, which is also fired from a direct ground emplacement and can be used to engage targets as close as 300m.

The operator can fire the Mamba from a remotely sited position up to 120m away from point of launch. He can use his control unit to vector the missile through 45 degrees after launch to engage a different target should he lose the first designated target. The Mamba can be fitted with two types of warhead, which can be either depot fitted or fitted in the field by trained operators. The first type is the standard HEAT warhead for anti-

tank roles. The second type available is the AT-FRAG which will penetrate up to 350mm of armour or can be used against personnel and soft-skinned vehicles in the open.

The Cobra and Mamba missiles are both designed to be fired directly from the ground, in a jump-launch sequence, without any launch rails, but vehicle-mounted versions can be adapted to use with special launcher rails.

The Pakistani Army is also known to have at least 800 of these missiles in war stock.

	Cobra	Mamba
Weight:	10.3kg	11.2kg
Length:	900mm	955mm
Body diameter:	100mm	120mm
Span:	480mm	400mm
Range min/max:	400m/2,000m	300m/2,000m
Speed:	300km/h	505km/h
Guidance:	MCLOS	SACLOS
Penetration (HEAT):	500mm	475mm

The programme to develop the Panzerfaust 3 anti-tank system for the then West German Army was started in 1978. It was decided to go for this system because it promised all-round capability against current and future MBTs, even against frontal armour and ERA.

The Panzerfaust 3 is a countermass RCL weapon, similar in function to the Armbrust. This allows the weapon to be operated from within confined spaces, making it ideal for use in combat situations in built-up areas. The HEAT warhead of the Panzerfaust 3 is oversized and allows for improvements to be incorporated into the weapon, such was the forward thinking of the design team.

The Panzerfaust 3 comprises of a reusable, shoulder-fired launcher into which various natures of projectiles can be loaded. These projectiles include multipurpose fragmentations rounds, HESH, smoke and illuminating as well as the dedicated HEAT anti-tank round. For use at night an Infra Red target marking system is incorporated into the sight unit. The warhead of the HEAT charge is 110mm calibre and will defeat

more than 700mm of armour to make it an extremely powerful weapon. It can be used to engage stationary targets out to 500m and against moving targets out to 300m range.

Like other powerful anti-tank weapons the Panzerfaust 3 has been developed into a range of remote firing, stand alone units. The Panzerfaust Off-Route Mine System is a typical stand-alone device using one launcher unit with an IR sensor and mounted on a tripod for siting off-route to cover the approaches along which an enemy vehicle may advance. The system detects the approach of a target MBT by means of an acoustic sensor, which in turn activates the IR sensor. This serves to activate the system's IR unit to determine the optimum engagement range of the target. Known more simply as the SIRA it is an all-weather, 24 hour a day system with a high degree of built-in fail-safe devices which render it immune to background noise, clutter and countermeasures. This system can engage targets out to 150m and remain active on its pair of 3.4 volt lithium cells for up to 40 days. The sensors will calculate engagement times for vehicles travelling at speeds between 30km/h and 60km/h.

A multiple launch version of the Panzerfaust 3 has been developed and is known as 'Fire Salamander'. This features four projectiles in a ready to fire state mounted on an autonomous tripod mount with a TV sensor.

The basic shoulder-fired Panzerfaust 3 launcher and ammunition can be carried by infantrymen deploying from APCs and helicopters. One man carries the launcher unit, in addition to his personal weapon, with other members of the combat section/squad carrying a number of reload rounds of different natures between them.

The Panzerfaust 3 is still in use with the German Army, following the re-unification of 1990.

Calibre:	110mm
Weight:	12.9kg
Length:	1.2m
Weight of projectile:	3.9kg
Range:	300m moving target,
	500m stationary target
Initial velocity:	163m/sec
Maximum velocity:	243m/sec
Time of flight:	1.36 seconds to 300m
Penetration:	700mm

GREECE

The 90mm EM67 is a lightweight recoilless weapon developed in Greece and is in current service with the Greek Army. It is a short-range, shoulder-fired weapon which can be fired from a support to aid stability when engaging moving vehicles. This is especially useful at longer engagement ranges. The telescopic sight has graticules to assist the firer in gauging aim-off against moving vehicles and the range to target.

The EM67 is a reusable weapon, and is reloaded via the rear breech mechanisim. This is operated by the weapon's number two operator, who works the action of a simple exterior-lug type system. It is served by two men, one to aim and fire with the second man to reload. It is fired by means of percussion and the HEAT round, which weighs 4.2kg, can be used to engage targets out to a practical range of 800m, although it will carry to 2,100m if the target is missed. Operating as a two-man tank/APC hunting team, deploying from either helicopters or APCs, both men would carry their individual weapon as well the EM67 launcher and spare rounds of ammunition

Calibre:	90mm
Length:	1,346mm
Weight:	16kg
Muzzle velocity:	220m/sec
Range:	800m effective, 2,100m maximum

IRAQ

Iraq was producing weapons of all natures long before the outbreak of the 1991 Gulf War following Iraq's invasion of Kuwait. Among one of the more basic weapons produced by the State Arsenals was the Iraqi copy of the well-known RPG-7 anti-tank grenade launcher, and known locally as the Al-Nassira. It is understood that this weapon has a basic tangent sight as opposed to the more detailed and accurate optical sight unit of the RPG-7. It is furthermore believed that the projectiles of the Al-Nassira are of the original RPG-7 pattern and not the improved two-stage motor type, nor are they believed to contain the improved design warheads. Therefore the use of the Al-Nassira would be restricted to light vehicles and weapon emplacements. It is in current use with the Iraqi Army.

Weight of launcher with sights:	7.4kg
Muzzle velocity:	120m/sec
Flight velocity:	300m/sec

ISRAEL

The B-300 Light Anti-Armour Weapon, or B-300 LAW, was designed and developed for the Israeli Army and actually appears in two versions, which is becoming an increasingly familiar feature with weapons of this nature. First there is the Mk.1 which has a projectile weight of 4.5kg and can penetrate 400mm of armour. Second is the Mk.2, which is heavier, with a HEAT projectile that can penetrate 550mm of armour.

The B-300 is similar in function to the French Army's LRAC 89mm, on which some sources claim it is based. Admittedly the B-300 features a reusable firing mechanism on to which the pre-loaded launch tube containing a HEAT projectile is clipped. After firing, the expended tube is removed and discarded. The fore-end of the B-300 with the firing mechanism can then be quickly reloaded with a new tube. This tube with the projectile is manufactured from glass reinforced plastic which makes it light in weight but very strong. It can be quickly and easily clipped onto the firing unit under all conditions, with the action of coupling making all the connections to ready the weapon for firing. The infantryman need not carry out any other procedures to use the weapon.

The projected mass of the HEAT round weighs 3.1kg on the Mk1 projectile and the heavier Mk.2 round features a high explosive follow through, HEFT, effect. Basically this is the Israeli version of the Tandem Warhead layout. The shaped charge of the Mk.2 round of the B-300 first blows a hole in the armour and the secondary charge follows close behind it. This weapon gives an infantryman the capability of engaging MBTs of all types, including those fitted with ERA.

The B-300 is a shoulder-fired weapon operated by a single infantryman. The firing unit and three rounds weigh only 19kg which means he can carry this load and still function as a basic infantryman in combat. Furthermore, he can still deploy from APCs or helicopters with this powerful load. If required for night operation, an illuminating round is available for firing from the B-300 firing unit. This has a brightness of around 600,000 candela and is effective out to a range of 1,700m. On firing the HEAT round has an initial velocity of 270m/sec and has an effective range of 400m.

The sight unit is integral with the reusable firing mechanism and contains a Betalight source for use in low light conditions. For covert night operations a passive night vision device can be clipped on to the B-300. A small bipod is also integral to the design of the weapon, and can be used by the firer to aid stability when tracking a moving target. The weapon can also be used in temperatures from -10 degrees to +60 degrees which allows reliability in desert conditions. It can be loaded and brought into action by a single infantryman in some 20 seconds.

Calibre:	82mm
Weight of launcher:	3.65kg
Weight loaded:	8kg
Length of launcher unloaded:	755mm
Length of launcher loaded:	1,400mm
Weight of projectile:	4.5kg
Length of projectile:	725mm
Initial muzzle velocity:	420m/sec
Range:	400m
Penetration:	400mm for Mk.1 and
	550mm for Mk.2 HEAT rounds

The Israeli MAPATS, or Man-Portable Anti-Tank System, exhibits features of both the Sagger and US TOW anti-tank systems. Indeed, on first sight it appears to be no more than an Israeli version of the TOW. Like TOW, the MAPATS is a heavyweight anti-tank missile which comes in a pre-loaded glass-fibre launching tube. However, there the direct similarity ends because the MAPATS is a laser beam-riding system and not SACLOS guided.

The target illuminating laser beam originates from the firer's control post. Such a guidance system is relative immune to jamming by countermeasures, and as long as the operator can see his target and illuminate it with the laser beam he will successfully engage it.

The MAPATS breaks down into four component parts: the pre-loaded launch tube, tripod, traverse and guidance system, and a night vision unit. After firing, the empty tube is discarded and a replacement can be quickly fitted, similar to the TOW. The missile has a range of 5,000m with a flight time 19.5 seconds out to 4,000m range. There is no reason to suppose that MAPATS could not be mounted on carrier vehicles in the same way as TOW and other heavyweight missiles. In this case the laser designator could be incorporated into the fire unit on the vehicle. In fact, the missile could also be helicopter mounted with either the launching helicopter or an escorting machine using a laser beam to illuminate the target.

The MAPATS is a crew-served weapon with a time into action of two minutes. This might seem slow, but for a long-range, heavy weapon this is better than might be imagined. It has a full 360 degree traverse and can be elevated between -20 degrees and +30 degrees. The warhead of the missile contains a 3.6kg HEAT charge that will penetrate 800mm of armour. This means MAPATS is capable of defeating all types of MBTs in current service, including those fitted with ERA.

Calibre:	148mm
Missile length:	1.45m
Missile weight:	18.5kg
Launch velocity:	70m/sec
Flight velocity:	315m/sec
Maximum range:	5000m
Weight of missile in container:	29.5kg
Weight of night vision unit:	6kg
Weight of traverse unit:	25kg
Weight of tripod and battery:	14.5kg

ITALY

Folgore is the name applied to the Italian Army's light, recoilless, shoulder-fired anti-tank weapon which is crewed by two men. Capable of being used to engage targets out to 1,000m, the Folgore can be used equally well against targets as close as 50m. A small tripod is supplied for crews engaging targets at ranges over 500m, which is required for accuracy.

The Folgore is an 80mm calibre reusable weapon but is today probably best only used against light armoured vehicles, such as APCs, rather than attempting to destroy an MBT, particularly if the target is equipped with ERA or other composite armour. However, it might still be powerful enough to inflict an 'M' kill or mobility kill on such an MBT.

In the tripod mounted version of the Folgore, one man serves to load the weapon and the firer uses an optical-electronic clip-on sight unit to view the target and take up the range. This particular type of mounting can be used from behind cover in either the prone or squat position. In the shoulder-fired version, the crew serves the weapon in the same way, but the firer uses a simplified optical sight. Depending on the level of cover available, the crew can assume a kneeling, standing or prone position to fire the Folgore from the shoulder.

The projectile is 80mm in calibre and carries a HEAT warhead. Each round weighs 5.2kg and is 740mm in length, which allows the two-man crew to carry several rounds between them in addition to personal weapons. The two-man crew with the Folgore can operate in the normal manner of infantry deploying from either APCs or helicopters. However there is no reason why a two-man crew with Folgore could not be motorised with a light wheeled vehicle to carry a number of reload rounds for the launcher, and engage targets of opportunity such as light APCs or static positions.

Calibre:	80mm
Muzzle velocity:	380m/sec
Overall length:	1.8m
Weight tripod version:	27kg
Weight shoulder-fired version:	17kg
Range:	50m to 1,000m

JAPAN

The Japanese-developed KAM-3 anti-tank missile programme was started for the Japanese Ground Self Defence Force as long ago as 1957. Howver, it was not introduced into service until 1964. Today, more than 30 years after introduction, the missile is still in service. This has been made possible through a series of upgrades to this otherwise basic MCLOS guided missile. In service with the JSDF it is known as the Type 64 and some 220 examples are still in frontline category. The Type 64, or KAM-3, has a cylindrical body and is stabilised by means of four fins laid out in cruciform pattern, which is very much standard on this form of missile system.

The Type 64's control surfaces have full-width spoilers and the missile contains a flare for the operator to track its path through his optical sight and guide it by means of a small thumb-operated joystick mounted on the control box. During night operations the operator can sight on the missile's rocket exhaust signature.

The Type 64 is crew-served by three men who place it on a basic metal frame angled to 15 degrees for launching in its ground role. On launching the missile is boosted by a rocket motor, after which a sustainer motor cuts in to provide a cruise speed of 85m/sec in less than one second. The Type 64 missile can be deployed from 4x4 light wheeled vehicles, which can carry up to four missiles. It can also be fired from helicopters, mounted on launch rails either side of the airframe. The Type 64 can be fired as a single missile or from multiple units. The missile is used only by the Japanese Self Defence Force.

Body diameter:	120mm
Span:	600mm
Length:	1,015mm
Weight at launch:	15.7kg
Speed:	85m/sec
Range min/max:	350m/1,800m

The KAM-9 anti-tank missile is another locally-developed weapon and is in service only with the Japanese Ground Self-Defence Force. It has been designed to be an all-round improvement over the older KAM-3, which it serves to augment in service.

The KAM-9 is a SACLOS guided missile fired from a pre-loaded launch tube mounted on a tripod firing post onto which is mounted the optical unit for target acquisition and through which the operator can make mid-course corrections. These corrections are transmitted to the missile by the usual SACLOS method – along the trailing wire to the missile's on-board computer. A solid-propellant booster ejects the missile from its launch tube, after which the stabilising fins deploy and the solid-fuel sustainer motor cuts in to boost it to cruising speed.

The KAM-9 is mid-way betwwen the Milan and TOW systems, and in that respect it is classed as manportable despite the fact that it is some 1,700mm in length. The exact details of the KAM-9 have still not yet been fully released by the Japanese, however it is understood that the it has a HEAT warhead and can be fired either directly by the operator or remotely, in which case it can be sited as multiple launching units. The in-built tracking flare is IR to permit the operator to observe the missile all the way to the target.

As with all Japanese-developed weapons the KAM-9 is not used by any overseas forces and is solely in service with the J6SDF.

Length of container:	1,700mm
Length of missile:	1,500mm
Container diameter:	200mm
Missile diameter:	150mm
Missile span:	330mm
Range:	3,000m to 4,000m

PAKISTAN

106mm RCL   67

The 106mm RCL in service with the Pakistan Army is essentially a locally developed version of the US-designed M40A1 RCL, also of 106mm calibre. The weapon comprises the M40A1 barrel, the Mount M79, the M8C spotting rifle and the M92F Elbow Telescope on the M90 Telescope Mount and the M42 Instrument Light. The spotting rifle is bought in from an outside source in Spain. This is used to range on the target in the same way as other RCLs.

This RCL of the Pakistan Army can be towed on its two-wheeled carriage behind a light vehicle under normal conditions, but it is possible to mount the weapon in the rear of a light wheeled vehicle in the same manner as other countries employ their RCLs. This still gives a full 360 degree traverse for target engagement with the HEAT rounds, which have a range of just over 2,000m in the direct fire role. In the indirect fire role the weapon has a range of 7,680m. It is served by a crew of four and when vehicle-mounted it can serve in the mobile anti-tank role with weapon, crew and ammunition being transported in one vehicle.

Calibre:	106mm
Weight of weapon:	115kg
Weight of mount:	82kg (M79)
Range:	2012m (maximum direct fire)
Muzzle velocity:	507m/sec

RUSSIA

The SPG-9 is a Russian weapon of ageing design, operating on the recoilless principle and firing fin-stabilised HEAT ammunition. The SPG-9 is a crew-served weapon operated by four men and fired from a tripod mount. For transportation it can be towed by a light vehicle using a two-wheeled carriage. The SPG-9 can be broken down into two man-portable loads: the tripod at 12kg and the launcher at 47.5kg. This means it can be used to equip the specialised anti-tank platoons operating with motorised rifle battalions and deploying from APCs such as BTR vehicles. However the 47.5kg launcher would require at least two men to handle it easily.

The propellant charge of the round is formed in a case that clips to an attachment behind the stabilising fins of the round, and gives it the appearance of an elongated mortar round. Only when the integral rocket motor initiates, at 20m away from the muzzle, does the velocity of the round increase to 700m/sec. The HEAT round is spin stabilised, the spin being imparted by means of a series of offset holes in the launching charge.

The SPG-9 has a low profile when deployed and two men can easily carry the barrel from one firing position to another. Due to its ability to be broken down into man-portable loads the SPG-9 can be manhandled over very rough terrain and sited in well prepared defensive positions in support of units that might otherwise be limited in their anti-tank capabilities.

Calibre:	73mm
Weight of launcher:	47.5kg
Weight of tripod:	12kg
Overall length:	2,110mm
Overall height on tripod:	900mm
Maximum range:	1,300m
Armour penetration:	390mm
Muzzle velocity:	700m/sec with rocket booster

The ammunition of the Russian-designed B-11 RCL has the appearance of elongated mortar rounds, in much the same style as the smaller SPG-9 RCL. The HEAT and HE rounds of the B-11 weigh 9kg and 13.6kg respectively, with the HEAT round capable of penetrating 380mm of armour at ranges up to 450m. The B-11 RCL has the added advantage in that it can be used to fire the HE rounds in the indirect role out to 6,650m. This allows it to act as very light field artillery to engage troops and light soft-skinned vehicles in the open. However the effectiveness and accuracy of the weapon in this role would be open to speculation.

The B-11 is towed on a two-wheeled carriage, and fired from a tripod mount, but in an emergency can be fired from the wheeled carriage. The weapon has been declared obsolete but according to reliable sources it is to still be found in the armouries of several countries around the world. It is a multi-vented breech block RCL weapon with an enlarged chamber section, which gives the B-11 the appearance of being a large version of the B-10 82mm RCL. Those countries that do still use the B-11 will find its light weight and relatively compact design useful to heliborne troops who could carry it as either an underslung load or internal cargo.

Calibre:	107mm
Overall length:	3.314m
Weight:	305kg
Anti-tank range:	450m
Armour penetration:	380mm
Rate of fire:	6 rounds per minute

Amazing as it might seem, a country with a powerful military force like Russia's still finds a place to deploy anti-tank guns in this missile age. In fact Russia deploys anti-tank guns in two calibres, 85mm and 100mm. There are two guns in the 100mm range, known as the M-1955 and T-12, both described as being anti-tank/field guns. Their capability in the anti-tank role is very much in doubt. Beyond engaging light AFVs, such as APCs, there is not much call for them on the battlefield. However, the light weight of these towed weapons does make them useful in the airborne role where they could be sited to complement more powerful anti-tank weapon systems such as guided missiles.

The T-12 gun is stated as being a high performance anti-tank weapon and can fire different natures of ammunition including HEAT, armour piercing discarding sabot (APDS), and armour piercing high explosive (APHE). The ordinary HE round can be fired out to 15,400m when it is deployed in the field gun role. The ammunition is of the fixed type, that is to say it is a complete round and does not use separate bagged charges. The APDS round has a muzzle velocity of 1,500m/sec and can be fired out to 8,500m.

The T-12 and the M-55 both operate with semi-automatic, vertical-sliding wedge breech-blocks to give a rate of fire of around eight to ten rounds per minute. The T-12 is the more modern weapon of the anti-tank gun range and has a barrel length of 84.84 calibres – it is 8.848m in length – and is a smoothbore weapon designed to fire fin-stabilised ammunition.

Weight:	3000kg
Length:	9.16m
Width:	1.7m
Height:	1.45m
Elevation:	-10 degrees to +20 degrees
Traverse:	27 degrees
Weight of projectile:	15.9kg (APHE)
Muzzle velocity:	1000m/sec (APHE)
Crew:	6

Despite being declared obsolete a weapon does not just disappear, and the M-1945 (D-44) is one such anti-tank gun. Introduced with the Russian Army towards the end of the Second World War it was subsequently taken up by some 20 other client states of the Russians. Although anti-tank guns are considered to be little if any tactical use on the modern battlefield, such guns are still to be found in some armies around the world.

There are actually two versions of this gun. One has a split trail and is held by airborne regimental anti-tank companies. The other is a self-propelled version used by motorised units. For mobility on the battlefield it has a small two-cylinder 14hp engine to move about at speeds up to 10kph across country.

Despite its age the D-44 can fire a comprehensive range of 85mm calibre ammunition apart from the obvious HEAT rounds for anti-tank roles. These other types of ammunition include armour piercing high explosive(APHE), high explosive(HE) and high velocity armour piercing (HVAP).

This weapon has a semi-automatic vertically sliding breech block of wedge design, which allows a high rate of fire to be achieved. Up to ten rounds per minute has been reported. This rate of fire is possible because the am-munition is of the fixed type, and not a separate bagged propellant charge and projectile. The rounds expended at this rate would not be particularly well aimed. If the shots were well aimed to engage a moving target at any distance one would expect this rate of fire to be much lower, at two or three rounds per minute.

Such a weapon would have limited value on the battlefield against modern main battle tanks, especially if they were fitted with ERA. Deployed with airborne forces, however, it could be used to engage any light AFVs that may be deployed against them in the reconnaissance role to assess their strengths.

Overall length:	8.2m
Width:	1.7m
Elevation:	-7 to +35 degrees
Projectile mass (HVAP):	5kg
Muzzle velocity (HVAP):	1030m/sec
Maximum range (HVAP):	1150m
Armour penetration (HVAP):	108mm at 1,000m range

The M-1955 towed anti-tank gun is the other specialised gun in service with the Russian Army in the 100mm calibre range. Dedicated primarily to the anti-tank role, it is the older of the two weapons. The M-1955 is a slightly heavier weapon than the T-12, but its overall dimensions are smaller. It is crewed by eight men, which is quite a large complement, and can be used to fire the main types of anti-tank round, including HVAP, HEAT and APHE. In its secondary role as light field gun, the M-1955 can fire HE shells of 15.7kg out to a maximum range of nearly 23,000m to engage infantry and light unarmoured vehicles, to harass and disrupt formations.

The barrel of the M-1955 is smoothbored and has a length of 54 calibres, that is to say 5,400mm in length. APHE shells are fired at a muzzle velocity of 1,000metres per second. It is fitted with a gun shield and a double baffle muzzle brake. The slightly more modern T-12 anti-tank gun, which is based on the M-1955, also has a gun shield but the muzzle brake is of the 'pepperpot' design.

The 100mm calibre HEAT round is capable of penetrating 380mm of armour at 1,000m range and the APHE, which weighs 15.9kg, will penetrate 185mm of armour at the same distance. The gun is fitted with a split trail and a two-wheeled carriage for towing behind a variety of prime mover vehicles. However, its relatively low weight allows it to be air transported in fixed wing aircraft such as the Antonov An-124 'Condor' or the Ilyushin Il-76, or carried underslung from medium lift helicopters.

Disregarding its vintage and battlefield limitations, the M-1955 anti-tank gun is still a useful weapon to have in a defensive position to counter both infantry and light armoured attacks.

Calibre:	100mm
Weight:	3300kg (travelling)
Weight:	3000kg (firing position)
Length:	8.72m
Width:	1.585m
Height:	1.89m
Elevation:	-10 to +45 degrees
Traverse:	55 degrees
Rate of fire:	10rpm max
Maximum range:	22,966m with HE
Muzzle velocity:	1,000m/sec with APHE

Considering that the B-10 RCL was declared obsolete from frontline service as long ago as 1985, it comes as no surprise to find that it still remains in service with the Russian Army. It is probably still used by a number of former satellite states also. The B-10 is a smooth-bored anti-tank weapon capable of firing fin-stabilised HEAT and HE rounds out to effective ranges of 400m and 4,500m respectively. The weapon is towed on a light two-wheeled carriage from which it is usually dismounted and re-assembled on a tripod for firing. However, in emergencies the B-10 can be fired from the wheeled carriage, which is fairly common practice with a weapon of this type. Its light weight of only 87.6kg allows the B-10 to be easily manhandled into position and it is a useful weapon with which to equip airborne forces to combat light reconnaissance vehicles.

This is a widely copied weapon, being the basis for the Chinese Type 65, for example. This particular RCL has a multi-vented breech-block with an enlarged breech section. The HE round weighs 4.5kg and with a muzzle velocity of 320m/sec and can engage targets out to 4,500m. This leads one to presume that the B-10 would only be used in this role when mortars or other light artillery is not available. The inherent inaccuracy of RCLs at great ranges would furthermore lead one to believe that such a method of target engagement is only for firing in the general direction of the target, such as troop concentrations in the open, to force them to seek cover.

The 82mm calibre HEAT round weighs 3.6kg and can be used against targets within a 400m range for effectiveness. The armour penetrating capability of the HEAT round is only 240mm which limits the B-10 to engaging light AFVs such as APCs and light wheeled vehicles. Troops operating from larger helicopters could carry the B-10 as either an internal cargo load or underslung, to allow it to be readied for use quicly when the troops deploy.

Calibre:	82mm
Barrel length:	1.659m
Overall length:	1.677m
Travelling weight:	87.6kg
Rate of fire:	6 to 7 rounds per minute

Without question the Russian RPG-7 is the most widely copied and widely used anti-tank weapon ever to be introduced into service. The number of client states purchasing this weapon in the past includes all the former Warsaw Pact members. Among those producing copies of the RPG-7 are China and Iraq, whose version is known as the Al Nassira (q.v.).

The RPG-7 is a shoulder-fired reloadable weapon, firing an 85mm calibre rocket with a HEAT warhead that is capable of penetrating 320mm of armour at 300m. The firer can usually carry spare rounds for the launcher in a simple satchel type carrier on his back, and other infantrymen in the unit can also carry spare rounds. Introduced in the 1960s, the RPG-7 has undergone many improvements to the projectile to increase its effectiveness, particularly the warhead and its fusing system. However, it still remains limited in its function due mainly to the fact that the weapon's maximum effective range is 300m at moving targets. The chances of it doing any real form of damage to modern MBTs is very remote. However, for use against light APCs and reconnaissance vehicles it does fulfil the role of anti-tank/vehicle weapon.

The RPG-7 has also been used by guerrilla forces around the world, including the Mujihadeen in Afghanistan, and even terrorist forces such as the IRA in Northern Ireland, who have used it with limited effect against armoured vehicles deployed on Internal Security operations with the British Army.

The optical sight for the weapon is clipped on to the launcher tube and there is provision for an IR sight for night operations. The rocket grenade itself is simply inserted into the front of the launcher until it lines up evenly with the firing mechanism, then the safety pin and nosecap are removed. The firer then has only to depress the trigger and the rocket is launched.

Accuracy is fairly good for a free-flight rocket of this type, but any form of side wind produces an erratic flight path. As with the Chinese version, the Type 69, there is a self-destruct range of 920m should it miss the target.

Its light weight and compactness lend the design of the RPG-7 to equipping troops of all roles, including airborne, motorised and infantry in the final assault phase of an attack, who can use it to destroy machine gun emplacements and mortar pits. As with other weapons of this nature, the RPG-7 has a severe backblast signature that prevents it from being used in enclosed spaces or near upright obstacles to the rear when firing.

Launcher tube calibre:	40mm
Projectile calibre:	85mm
Length of launcher tube:	990mm
Length of projectile:	620mm
Weight of launcher tube:	7kg
Weight of projectile:	2.25kg
Muzzle velocity:	300m/sec
Range:	300m moving target,
	500m static target

The Russian RPG-18 light anti-armour weapon is a virtual copy of the American-built M-72 LAW 66mm disposable weapon. Like that weapon, the RPG-18 is a telescopic, shoulder-fired weapon that is discarded after use. Its light weight of 4kg and folded length of only 705mm makes it an ideal weapon for an infantryman to use in a variety of ways, such as clearing machine gun emplacements, or blasting clearings through buildings during street fighting, as well as engaging light AFVs.

The launcher comes pre-loaded with a rocket, and unlocking the bayonet catch releases the two halves of the weapon to extend to its firing length of 1,000mm. The firing mechanism is mechanical and on extending the weapon for firing very basic sights, which are no more than a simple frame, pop up for the firer to engage the vehicle. A series of cartoon-like instructions is drawn on the side of the RPG-18 launcher tube. These are intended more as a quick reference guide in the field rather than in-depth weapon instruction. One of the illustrations warns the firer that the rear of the weapon should not be placed within two metres of a wall when firing.

The sights are graduated in increments of 50m range through to 200m range, which is comparable to most other weapons of this design. The compact design of the RPG-18 means each man in a section/squad operating from an APC could be equipped with at least one launcher for use against softer targets. The same would apply when deploying from helicopters, or special forces such as airborne or amphibious troops.

Calibre:	64mm
Length folded:	705mm
Length extended:	1,000mm
Weight:	4kg
Projectile weight:	2.5kg
Penetration of armour:	250mm to 300mm
Combat range:	200mm
Muzzle velocity:	114m/sec

The Russian-designed and built AT-2 'Swatter' is one of the earliest of a range of anti-tank missiles known as 'first generation'. Using Manual Command to Line Of Sight, MCLOS, the AT-2, known to NATO by the reporting name of Swatter, was, and indeed still is, used from a firing platform mounted on a vehicle such as the BRDM range of AFVs. The Swatter was used by the Egyptian Army with devastating effect against Israeli tanks during the Middle East War in 1967.

Rather bulky in form, the Swatter is usually mounted in banks of four on launch rails fitted to the deck of the carrying vehicle. The optical sight allows the operator to control the missile's flight to its target from under cover of the vehicle's armour by means of a small joystick control. The missile weighs 26.5kg and carries a large hollow-charge warhead capable of penetrating between 400mm and 500mm of armour.

The Swatter has four stabilising fins laid out in cruciform pattern and has a closing speed of 540km/h out to a range of 2,500m. It is capable of being mounted on helicopters such as the Mi-24, which can carry four missiles in additional to its other armament. The design of the Swatter's nose cone suggests some form of IR terminal seeker head. The operator can maintain visual contact with the Swatter by means of two tracking flares located on a pair of the stabilising fins that govern the missile's course corrections, allowing him to gather the missile into his sight unit for guidance.

Weight at launch:	26.5kg
Length of missile:	1,130mm
Diameter:	130mm
Span:	660mm
Rocket motor:	Solid fuel
Guidance:	MCLOS
Range:	600m to 2,500m
Armour penetration:	400mm to 500mm

As with the AT-2 'Swatter', the AT-3 was combat tested during the Middle East war of 1973, when troops of the Egyptian Army used it to inflict heavy casualties against Israeli tanks. First observed in May 1965 and given the NATO reporting name of Sagger, it is another 'first generation' guided anti-tank weapon, being of Manual Command to Line Of Sight, MCLOS. On firing a multi-core cable unspools from the missile and course corrections are passed to the missile in the form of MCLOS commands from the operator.

Weight at launch:	11.3kg
Length:	880mm
Diameter:	120mm
Span:	380mm
Range:	500m to 3,000m
Average velocity:	120m/sec
Armour penetration:	400mm +

It weighs 11.3 kg and can be operated by infantry using a special ground emplaced launcher, which has been described as being similar to a suitcase. Sagger can also be platform mounted to fire from either a single rail launcher or a retractable multiple launcher system on the range of BRDM or BTR AFVs. In the anti-tank helicopter role up to four Sagger missiles can be carried on helicopters such as the Mi-24, in addition to other weaponry.

On firing the missile is accelerated by a boost motor that has nozzles placed just behind the warhead. After this initial phase the Sagger then cruises on a solid fuel sustainer motor out to a maximum range of 3,000m. The Sagger lacks aerodynamic controls, being roll stabilised, with a tracking flare to allow the operator to steer the missile on to the target. It is unusual in that targets engaged between 500m and 1,000m are guided without the aid of optical sights, but beyond these ranges the operator gathers the missile on to a line above the target and steers it through the 10x magnification periscopic sight.

Unusually for a missile of this nature, Sagger does not come as a complete round ready to use when deployed by infantry. The HEAT warhead, which is piezo-electrically fused, has to be clipped on to the main body housing the sustainer motor when preparing it for firing. On vehicle mounted launcher rails the Sagger is already assembled.

Known as 'Spigot' to NATO forces, the Russian-built AT-4 ATGW has been in service for a number of years, equating roughly in terms to the Milan. The AT-4 is a high-performance, tube-launched anti-tank missile that uses SACLOS guidance and is used extensively by former client and satellite states of Russia. An infantry weapon, the Spigot was not widely known to the West until 1980 when details began to emerge. The system uses a similar layout to Milan, in that it comprises of a pre-loaded launching tube, firing post and sight unit containing the electronics for the SACLOS guidance. A two-man crew serves the weapon, one man acting as the operator and the second man to reload a launcher tube on the firing post's rails.

With a maximum range of 2,500m target engagement, the Spigot has a 25% increase in range over the Milan. At ranges of 2,000m the Spigot is credited with a hit rate greater than 90% at static targets. The warhead is a HEAT charge, weighing 3kg, and is understood to be capable of defeating 500mm to 600mm of armour at an angle of 90 degrees. The overall weight of the system is some 40kg with the pre-loaded launching tube weighing about 12kg alone. It was the appearance of this system that led NATO observers to conclude that

SACLOS guidance was entering service with the Russian Army and would begin to replace the older MCLOS guidance methods of older anti-tank missiles, such as the 'Snapper', 'Swatter' and 'Sagger' systems.

Warhead diameter:	120mm
Diameter of launch tube:	135mm
Length of launch tube:	1200mm
Maximum range:	2,000m to 2500m
Time of flight to maximum range:	11 sec
Velocity:	180 to 200m/sec
Armour penetration:	500mm to 600mm

This is another Russian anti-tank missile that was unknown to NATO until observed during the 1977 Red Square parade in Moscow. This vehicle-mounted anti-tank weapon has been given the NATO reporting name of 'Spandrel' and is yet another Russian system that obviously owes its origins to the Milan. This tube-launched system has a blow-out front closure and a flared tail which allows efflux from the boost charge to pass through. The Spandrel is mounted on roof-mounted quadruple rail launchers fixed to vehicles such as BMPs and BRDMs. Such a method of platform-mounting gives the system a full 360 degree traverse for target engagement and make the most use of this long-range system which can engage targets out to 4,000m with SACLOS guidance. In the BRDM vehicle-mounted role there is sufficient room in the interior of the vehicle to allow for some 15 reload missiles to be carried.

The exact capability of the Spandrel's armour penetration is uncertain, but it has to be gauged that its HEAT warhead has to be comparable to the shorter range Spigot which is 500mm to 600mm. The operator can control the missile's flight from under cover of the carrying vehicle's protective hull. When mounted on the BRDM range of AFVs, five Spandrel missiles are carried on a launcher frame with reload missiles carried inside the vehicle. On the BMP range of AFVs a single Spandrel launcher tube is mounted on the roof of the turret with further reload missiles carried internally. This gun/missile mix permits the crew of the vehicle to engage different target types at varying ranges.

Diameter of launcher:	135mm
Length of launcher:	1,200mm
Launcher weight:	10kg to 12kg
Maximum range:	4,000m
Maximum velocity:	175m/sec

The Kornet AT-14 anti-tank guided missile is the latest system to emerge from Russia and was first seen as recently as 1994 at a major defence exhibition. The Kornet is understood to be a laser beam-riding system – a reliable method of guiding missiles towards their targets. However, the drawback to illuminating targets by laser is the possibility that they may carry laser illuminating warning systems, such as the British Army's 'Saviour' device. This warns the crew they are being scanned by lasers and automatically brings the main armament of the vehicle to bear on the source of the laser. Despite this, laser guidance remains immune to counter-measures and as long as the system operator can see the target and illuminate it with a laser the weapon will strike the target.

Kornet is stated as having an engagement range of targets between 100m and 5,500m, and can be fired from a launching post by infantry or platform mounted on either light or armoured vehicles. It is understood the Kornet is to replace the ageing AT-5 'Spandrel', which will no doubt continue in service for some time after the full introduction into service of the Kornet.

The new system has a tripod, which weighs 19kg, for infantry use. The launch tube is pre-loaded and weighs 27kg and the thermal imager weighs 11kg. Such weights lend the missile to vehicle launching rather than use by infantry units. Guidance is by SACLOS, with four fins on the tail in cruciform layout imparting spin for stability, and a pair of canard fins towards the warhead which are used for course corrections.

The warhead contains a shaped or HEAT charge that is understood to be very powerful and capable of defeating explosive reactive armour. In addition to its anti-tank role there are versions of the Kornet fitted with warheads containing fuel-air explosives, sometimes referred to as either volumetric or thermobaric explosive. This particular version would be used against buildings, infantry in the open or defended strongpoints that are protected with a sandbag covering.

When it is fired the operator simply locks the illuminating laser onto the target and the Kornet will fly down the beam to strike the target. Still very much in the early days of production at the time of writing, the

Kornet has yet to enter full service with the Russian Army. It should be noted that Kornet is the name given to this missile system by the Russians themselves and it has yet to be granted a NATO reporting name.

Missile diameter:	152mm
Length of missile:	1,200mm
Weight of tripod launcher:	19kg
Launch tube with missile:	29kg
Weight of TI sight:	11kg
Range:	100m to 5,500m

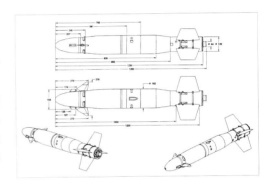

SOUTH AFRICA

FT-5   83

The South African Self-Defence Force has the locally developed FT5 weapon in current service for anti-tank purposes. It is a shoulder-fired weapon comprising a reusable forward section containing the sight unit and firing mechanism, and the disposable, pre-loaded launch tubes. This design makes it comparable in action to the Israeli B-300 and American SMAW.

There are currently three types of projectile available for use with the FT5, all in pre-loaded tubes. First is the standard HEAT round which can penetrate 650mm of armour. Second is the HEAT/RA which is a tandem warhead and can defeat 630mm of armour even when protected by ERA. Last is the HE Multi-purpose round which can defeat 500mm of concrete, sandbagged positions or penetrate more than 40mm of steel plate.

The sight unit of the FT5 is a x4 magnification unit containing all the usual graticule layouts associated with such an optical device dedicated to a shoulder-fired anti-tank weapon. An image-intensifier unit can be clipped on for night operations. The action of clipping the pre-loaded launch tubes to the firing unit creates the couplings for operational readiness. The missile becomes armed only when it is between 20m to 40m away from point of firing for safety purposes.

The FT5 is quite bulky and lengthy, but no more so than other weapons of a comparable design, and is too important to be overlooked as an infantryman's anti-tank weapon. It is operated by one man, but a second man in attendance would serve to carry reload tubes for the FT5 to allow continuous target engagement. In its unloaded state the FT5 can be carried by infantrymen operating from APCs and helicopters.

The FT5 launcher can be used against targets between 40m and 400m under normal conditions, but with accurate rangefinding this can be increased to 600m with little or no degradation of effect on the target.

Calibre:	92mm
Length of launcher:	1,050mm
Length of projectile:	780mm
Weight of launcher empty:	5.4kg
Weight in loaded condition:	11.3kg
Range:	40m to 400m
Muzzle velocity (HEAT):	275m/sec
Penetration (HEAT):	650mm

SPAIN

The M-65 weapon was developed for the Spanish Army by a local company and is in the unusual calibre of 88.9mm. The M-65 is a shoulder-fired, reusable weapon that can be telescopically collapsed for ease of carrying. It uses an electromagnetic firing mechanism that is automatically linked to the round when it is loaded. The M-65 has a bipod attached for stability when engaging moving targets, and the sight unit has an adjustable light source to illuminate the aiming graticules for night operations.

There are three types of ammunition available. The FIM66 round is a smoke projectile weighing 2.7kg that can be fired out to a range of 1,300m for screening purposes to cover the advance of troops or vehicles. It can also be used to 'mark' a target site for engaging with artillery or mortars. The MB66 round is a dual-purpose projectile that can be used to engage personnel and light unarmoured vehicles in the open. This round weighs 2.9kg and is capable of penetrating 250mm of armour at 300m range but has a maximum range of 1,000m, a distance which makes it useful as a harassment weapon against infantry in the process of deploying for an assault. The dedicated anti-tank round is the CHM81L, which weighs 2.3kg and will penetrate 430mm of armour at ranges up to 450m.

Calibre:	88.9mm
Length:	850mm (folded),
	1,640mm (firing order)
Weight of launcher:	6kg
Range for anti-tank round:	450m
Initial velocity for anti-tank round:	215m/sec

The Spanish Alcotan anti-tank system is at present in an advanced state of development. From details released by the manufacturers it appears to be similar to the American SMAW, Israeli B-300 and French LRAC 89mm. The front section is a reusable launcher unit containing the firing mechanism and to which is clipped, by means of a simple bayonet fitting, a pre-loaded tube containing a projectile with a HEAT charge capable of penetrating 600mm of armour. Unlike the other systems mentioned above, the Alcotan sight unit is very advanced for a weapon of this type. It contains an in-built laser rangefinder and a ballistic computer to calculate the speed and determine the range of the target. A bright spot is projected onto the target, which is visible through the sight unit, and the in-built computer calculates the amount of lead or aim-off the firer needs to take against a moving target. It is understood that HE/FRAG projectiles are being developed as well as the HEAT rounds, and a HEDP round is being considered for use against bunkers and buildings. It is quite a heavy weapon but this is off-set by the fact that it can engage MBT targets out to 500m, with the projectile capable of carrying out to 1,200m.

Calibre:	100mm
Length of reusable unit:	580mm
Length in firing mode (Loaded):	1.350m
Weight in firing condition:	13kg
AT Range:	500m
Launch velocity:	28m/sec
Penetration:	600mm
Hole diameter:	300mm

The Aries anti-tank system is another Spanish-American consortium-produced weapon, comprising of input from one leading American company and three Spanish companies. The technical know-how is provided by the American company and the three Spanish companies will provide the full development and production of the Aries missile system for the Spanish army. The missile programme is understood to be at present in an advanced state of development. The Aries is designed to be a man-portable system guided by means of a SACLOS unit. It is a tube-launched weapon fired from a tripod on which the optical and guidance units are also mounted. It is understood that Aries will have a high degree of lethality against all current MBTs in service and will be highly resistant to electronic counter-measures, ECM. The system will have a weight of about 15.9kg and a total length around 1,000mm. Aries will be capable of being deployed with heliborne troops or infantrymen operating from APCs. Aries will be capable of engaging targets between 65m and 2,000m, with a flight time of 4.5 seconds out to 1,000m and 8.5 seconds out to 2,000m. This gives it a faster time of flight than Milan.

Calibre:	148.6mm
Length:	1016mm
Weight complete:	11.4kg
Range:	65m to 2,000m

Consortiums to produce weapons of all types are now becoming a common policy between companies with a similar goal in mind. In the field of anti-tank weapons this is perhaps more common than any other form of weapon development. For example both the HOT and Milan anti-tank missile systems began as a Franco-German consortium and subsequently were widely adapted for service use. MACAM-3 is a classic example. Designed in co-operation between the American company of Hughes Aircraft and the Spanish company of Gyconsa, the MACAM-3 is being developed under contract with the Spanish Ministry of Defence.

The MACAM-3 is a shoulder-fired third generation anti-tank missile offering major improvements in operational effectiveness, reliability and battlefield survivability over comparable weapons. The MACAM-3 is a multi-purpose weapon, being capable of engaging AFVs, bunkers and hovering helicopters. By using fibre optic data link technologies the weapon will give the infantryman full 'fire and forget' capability, but remains highly flexible.

The MACAM-3 is still very much in its early programme stages, so exact details are unavailable. Rather than present misleading specifications it has been decided to simply describe the MACAM-3 without dimensions.

What is known is that MACAM-3 will have an engagement range between 200m and 2,500m with an IR seeker in the warhead, and a tandem charge to defeat reactive armour. Being of the ACLOS design it can lock on before launch or lock on after launch to engage the target. Further developments are already looking at remote firing posts and vehicle mounted versions, which should allow target engagements out to 5,000m.

This particular model of the 106mm recoilless rifle is the Spanish version of the ubiquitous American-designed M40A1, built under licence. This is a popular design of recoilless weapon and is widely made or copied. This Spanish version is a particularly well made example of the weapon and is identical to the original American design. It is fitted with an optical aiming sight and the usual 12.7mm calibre spotting rifle to aid range indication and when mounted on a tripod for firing it has a full 360 degree traverse. However, it can be adapted for use from a variety of vehicle platforms, such as light, unarmoured wheeled vehicles, to provide mobility on the battlefield. In fact this is a favoured option of mounting and using any RCL of this type. The Spanish 106mm RCL can be elevated to 27 degrees over the tripod mount, but with the venturi between the support legs it can be elevated to 65 degrees, which allows it fire the anti-personnel round out to ranges in excess of 7,600m. It can be depressed to -17 degrees. This makes it useful for use in mountainous terrain where the gun might be sited above the path of an oncoming vehicle to fire down onto the less well armoured roof. The Spanish 106mm RCL can fire the usual HEAT ammunition to engage vehicles and an anti-personnel round is also available for engaging infantry in the open. A crew of three operates this weapon but two men can still engage targets if necessary.

Overall length:	3.40m
Height on tripod:	1.13m
Weight:	219kg
Muzzle velocity:	503m/sec
Maximum range:	7640m

The C-90 anti-tank weapon of the Spanish Army actually comprises a series of six different disposable, shoulder-fired weapons. Five of this series are dedicated to the anti-tank role, of which two have the secondary anti-personnel role, and the sixth weapon being a smoke incendiary projectile. Rather than list the merits and specifications of each weapon individually, which would make for very repetitive reading, a list has been attached to the end of this entry for easier reference. Each weapon in the series comes as a pre-loaded projectile contained in a glass reinforced plastic launch tube. The firing mechanism is pyrotechnic, which makes for a reliable method of launching. Each weapon is equipped with a x2 magnification sight, allowing the C-90 weapons to be used in their anti-tank roles at optimum ranges between 250m for moving targets and out to 400m for stationary targets. The warheads of the C-90 anti-tank weapons are true HEAT charges. The two not fully anti-tank types are dual-purpose HEAT-FRAG, to allow infantry and soft targets to be engaged. For night operations the sight unit contains a permanent light source to allow target engagement in low light level conditions. The calibre for the whole series is 90mm. The weight never exceeds 5.5kg and the length is never more than 940mm. This makes the C-90 series a suitable weapon system for troops deploying from APCs, helicopters or operating in amphibious warfare or other special forces roles. For the size of the projectiles in the C-90 series they are extremely powerful, even in the anti-personnel role where the dual-purpose warheads have a lethal radius of 21m. The C-90 represents a comprehensive range of weaponry. Each man in an infantry combat squad/section could in effect carry a different example of the C-90 series to allow the section to react to individual situations as they arise.

	C90-C	C90-C-AM	C90-CR	C90-CR-RB	C90-CR-AM	C90-CR-FIM
Role:	AT	AT/AP	AT	AT	AT/AP	Smoke/Incendiary
Length:	840mm	840mm	940mm	940mm	940mm	940mm
Weight:	4.2kg	4.2kg	4.8kg	4.8kg	4.8kg	5.35kg
Penetration: (steel)	400mm	220mm	400mm	500mm	220mm	-
Penetration: (concrete)	1,000mm	650mm	1,000mm	1,200mm	650mm	-
Range AT:	200m	200m	300m	300m	300m	-
Range AP:	-	600m	-	-	800m	750m
AP Fragments:	-	>1,000	-	-	>1000	-
Lethal radius:	-	21m	-	-	21m	-

SWEDEN

This Swedish-designed weapon is in universal use, even being found in some armies where the equipment is an admixture of Russian and Western in origin. Indeed, this is one of the few weapons not developed by Japan or of non-American influence to be used by the Japanese Ground Self Defence Forces. The 84mm Carl Gustav was developed as a medium anti-tank weapon, MAW, and has been used extensively in that role during several conflicts. With a fierce backblast area it is limited to use in open spaces and can fire several natures of ammunition ranging from HEAT rounds to smoke. During the opening phases of the Argentinian invasion of the Falkland Islands, which led to the Falklands War with Britain in 1982, the 84mm Carl Gustav was used by a Royal Marine to engage the Argentinian Corvette 'Guerico' as it approached the harbour at Grytviken. He succeeded in hitting it with at least three rounds and forcing it to withdraw. There is also an account that during the same incident the Carl Gustav was used to engage and destroy an approaching helicopter. At present the Carl Gustav is available in the older M2 version made from light alloy and weighing 14.2kg, and the more modern M3 version, which is manufactured from a thin

steel liner barrel reinforced by filament wound carbon fibre laminate and weighs only 8.5kg. Both versions operate on the percussion principle to fire the ammunition, which is a highly reliable method of initiating the projectiles. Both versions of the 84mm Carl Gustav are shoulder-fired and reusable, being served by a two-man crew: the operator and the 'number two' who loads the weapon and carries extra rounds. Other members of the section/squad to which the Carl Gustav is attached would be required to carry at least one round for the weapon, also. To prepare for firing the operator shoulders the weapon and cocks it by means of a thumb-operated mechanism and the safety is applied. The 'number two' serves the vent which he unlocks by operating the external lugs, and swings the venturi section away to allow a round to be inserted. A cut-out section allows him to index the round and align it with the striker mechanism, and the venturi is swung closed. The operator then acquires his target in the sight, releases the safety and squeezes the trigger which has a pistol-grip layout. The whole process can be accomplished by a well-trained crew in seconds. The telescopic sight is a simple clip-on unit with graticule lines to permit the

operator to gauge the range to the target. There are also permanent 'iron sights' attached to the launcher which give reasonable accuracy in an emergency. The standard HEAT round FFV551, weighs 3.2kg and will penetrate 400mm of armour at ranges up to 700. The HEDP round FFV502 can be used against buildings in fighting in built-up areas or against troops in the open. The weapon has a large backblast area and must be fired without obstacles or debris to the rear, but can be fired with screening cover to the front. The firer can adopt the kneeling, standing or prone position to fire, depending on the tactical situation at the time. Weighing 3.3kg the FFV502 round can penetrate 150mm of concrete at 500m range or be used to engage troops in the open at ranges out to 1000m. The HE round FFV441B contains a time fuse and some 800 steel balls to engage troops in the open at ranges up to 1100m with air bursts for greater effectiveness. This round can be used against light, unarmoured wheeled vehicles with good effect, also. Despite its age, for example the M2 version has been in service with the British Army since 1965, the 84mm Carl Gustav is still useful, due largely to ammunition improvements. The relevant specifications for the five main different natures of ammunition available for use with the Carl Gustav are given below. The Illuminating FFV 545 round can be fired out to a maximum range of 2,100m and will light up an area 400m

to 500m radius with 650, 000 candela of light, with a burn time of thirty seconds. The Smoke FFV 469B round contains an 800g titanium tetrachloride composition to produce smoke. This compound is non-toxic and non-destructive, unlike white phosphorous, and produces a screening effect instantaneously on impact out to ranges of 1300m. The ammunition for the Carl Gustav is a continuous improvement programme and can be used in temperatures ranging from sub-zero temperatures to desert conditions, and can also be used by amphibious troops. This combined with the fact that the weapon functions on the percussion system to initiate the ammunition, makes for a reliable weapon under all conditions and in all terrains. Indeed, because of this high degree of reliability and all-purpose uses there is no reason to assume that it is to be superseded by anything in the foreseeable or immediate future.

	M2	M3
Calibre:	84mm	84mm
Length:	1130mm	1070mm
Weight:	14.2kg	8.5kg

Telescopic Sight:	
Weight:	1kg
Magnification:	x2
Field of view:	17 degrees

Ammunition Types:

	FFV 551 HEAT	FFV 502 HEDP	FFV 441B HE	FFV 545 ILLUM	FFV 469B SMOKE
Weight of round:	3.2kg	3.3kg	3.1kg	3.1kg	3.1kg
Weight of shell:	2.4kg	2.5kg	2.3kg	2.2kg	2.2kg.
Muzzle velocity:	255m/s.	230m/s	240m/s	260m/s	240m/s
Armour penetration:	400mm	150mm	-	-	-
Arming range:	5-15m	15-40m	20-70m	-	-
Effective range:	700m	500m	1,100m	2,100m	1,300m

Although the AT-4 light anti-armour weapon was developed in Sweden for the Swedish Army, its usefulness has been widely recognised and it is now used extensively around the world. In fact, the AT-4 is manufactured under licence in the US for the US Army, where it is known as the M-136, and is a replacement for the ageing 66mm M72 LAW. Production started in 1986 and the AT-4 has been used in combat situations, most notably by troops of the US Coalition Forces during Operation Just Cause and Operation Desert Storm in the 1991 Gulf war against Iraq.

The AT-4 is a disposable, shoulder-fired weapon of simple design and simple functions. It comprises a glass-reinforced plastic launch tube, which is pre-loaded with a rocket fitted with a HEAT warhead. The launch tube contains all the required attachments for instant operational readiness, including sights, firing mechanism and safety features. An AT-4 launcher tube is fitted with a carrying strap to permit infantrymen to carry it in the slung position.

The firing sequence of the AT-4 is very straight-forward. The operator simply extracts the forward safety pin, unsnaps the shoulder rest, places it on his shoulder and releases the sights. He then arms the cocking lever, takes aim on his target, disengages the safety catch and fires the weapon. All this takes only seconds to perform and the controls are all at the operator's fingertips for ease of use. The AT-4 HEAT round will penetrate 420mm of armour, with behind armour effects, at ranges up to 300m. This acts in much the same manner as the SMAW HEDP, but in this case will destroy the internal systems of a vehicle and kill the crew with spall dragged in from the armour plate.

With a total weight of 6.7kg per launcher tube, it is possible to arm a full infantry section/squad with AT-4 launchers to engage vehicles or defeat emplaced machine gun positions protected with earth or sandbags. With an operating temperature range between -40C and +60C the AT-4 is an ideal weapon for equipping rapid deployment forces such as marines or airborne units, who have to operate in all climatic ranges.

Calibre:	84mm
Overall length:	1,000mm
Weight:	6.7kg
Weight of projectile:	3kg
Range:	300m
Armour penetration:	420mm
	(rolled homogeneous armour)
Muzzle velocity:	290m/sec

The RBS-56 anti-tank missile from Sweden is in use with several countries world-wide. It has the acronym 'BILL' which stands for Bofors Infantry Light and Lethal. Introduced into service in the mid-1980s, it falls into the same category of anti-tank missiles as the Milan and US-designed M-47 Dragon. It originated in response to a weapon capable of defeating composite armour. The development programme for BILL started in mid-1979, during which time the manufacturers and Swedish Army worked very closely with one another.

The HEAT warhead of BILL has a unique action. As it approaches its target a proximity fuse detects the tank and detonates the warhead at the optimum moment as it flies over the top of the vehicle. In other words the BILL attacks the top of the tank where the armour is at its thinnest. For this purpose the warhead is angled at 30 degrees and will penetrate the roof of the turret or rear engine decking, thereby side-stepping having to blast through ERA.

The missile flies about one metre above the operator's line of sight to place it higher and allow the top attack action to take place. The missile leaves the tube propelled by its booster motor, then a solid fuel sustainer motor cuts in for flight to target, and the stabilising cruciform fins deploy along with the control surfaces.

Calibre of missile:	150mm
Length:	900mm
Weight, missile in tube:	16kg
Weight of sight and firing post:	11kg
Range:	150m to 2,000m
Time of flight:	10 sec to 2,000m
Crew:	2
Deployment time:	20 sec
Reload time:	7 sec

BILL is SACLOS guided and has a full 24 hour capability of target engagement in all weather conditions. The missile system consists of three parts: the pre-loaded launch tube containing the missile, the firing post, and the sight unit. It is crew-served by two men who divide the load between them.

The missile is not mounted on helicopters, but it can be operated from vehicles mounting the firing post with additional reload missiles carried internally. The missile can be deployed for action in some twenty seconds with a reload time of just seven seconds, and can engage targets between 150m and 2,000m range. The full armour penetration capabilities of BILL are unclear, but it is believed to be capable of defeating all current ranges of MBTs due to the unique action of its warhead.

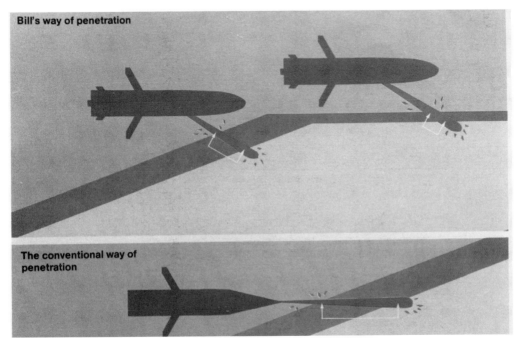

Bill's way of penetration

The conventional way of penetration

The 'Miniman' anti-tank launcher developed by Sweden is now obsolete, but is worth looking at out of curiosity because it influenced so many designs of disposable anti-tank weapons. For its time the Miniman was a very powerful, shoulder-fired disposable anti-tank weapon that was only ever used by the Swedish Army. It was of 74mm calibre and has been replaced in service by the 84mm Carl Gustav and AT-4 weapons. The Miniman weighed 2.9kg, of which the round weighed 0.88kg containing 0.3kg of explosives in the HEAT warhead. It was only 900mm in length which allowed an infantryman to carry two or three launchers in addition to his normal equipment.

The weapon could be used to engage targets out to 250m range and penetrate 300mm of armour. It had a muzzle velocity of 160m/sec and had to be used in conditions with a clear rear area because of the backblast. The compact disposable design of the Miniman set the benchmark for comparable weapons based on the design.

Type:	One shot disposable
Calibre:	74mm
Length:	900mm
Weight:	2.9kg
Warhead:	HEAT
Range:	250m
Penetration:	300mm

The PV-1110 RCL 90mm anti-tank weapon is currently in service with the Swedish Army and the Army of the Republic of Ireland, even though some sources declare it to be obsolete. It is known, however, to no longer be manufactured except for spare parts. However, weapons of this type are encountered more often than one might believe.

The PV-1110 can be mounted to fire from a light vehicle or fired directly from its two-wheeled carriage by which it is normally towed. In this role the weapon can be rotated about its axis on a turntable to permit traversing between 75 degrees and 115 degrees, depending on elevation, to engage targets.

A crew of three operates the weapon. It is quite powerful, considering its age, with a hollow charge warhead capable of penetrating 380mm of armour at a 90 degree incidence at ranges of 700m. For aiming purposes a special spotting rifle, with a ten round magazine of 7.62mm ammunition, is mounted on the barrel of the PV-1110. This is used in a similar way to the spotting rifle of the Wombat (qv).

The PV-1110 is claimed to be capable of six rounds per minute, but well-aimed shots would probably take this down to two or three rounds per minute. Both the Irish Republic and Sweden are non-aligned states, which may account for them being the only users of this Swedish designed weapon.

Calibre:	90mm
Muzzle velocity:	715m/sec
Overall length:	4,100mm
Barrel length:	3,700mm (41 calibres)
Width:	1,375mm
Height:	870mm
Weight:	260kg
Elevation:	-10 to +15
Weight of shell:	9kg, of which 3.1kg is the projectile
Muzzle velocity:	715m/sec
Range:	900m maximum

SWITZERLAND

The Swiss-developed Rocket Launcher 58/80 is an 83mm calibre reusable shoulder-fired anti-tank weapon specially developed for the Swiss Army, who is the only user state, and replaced the 83mm Rocket Launcher 58. The original design was based on the Belgian 'Blindicide' anti-tank weapon, also of 83mm calibre.

The Swiss 58/80 is a two-man weapon, aimed and fired by one man with the second serving as loader. Although rather bulky, it has a relatively low weight of 8.5kg for a weapon of this type. It features a carrying strap for the firer and a small frontal shield through which an observation slit is cut.

It is capable of engaging static targets out to 300m range with free-flight rockets carrying a HEAT warhead, and the crew can adopt the kneeling, standing or prone position when firing from behind cover. The 58/80 is rather old-fashioned in appearance but it serves the purposes of the Swiss Army. With its backblast area the weapon is limited to use in clear spaces with no obstacles or debris to the rear.

Calibre:	83mm
Length:	1,300mm
Weight:	8.5kg
Effective range:	200m against moving targets, 300m against static targets
Muzzle velocity:	100m/sec

According to reliable sources the Swiss Army still holds up to 850 examples of these towed anti-tank guns on its inventory. As obsolete as they may appear, their usefulness in the anti-tank role would not be in dispute during fighting in built-up areas, where they could hit the more vulnerable areas of the vehicle from very close range. Both the PAK 50 and PAK 57 are of 90mm calibre. They were introduced into service within a short space of time of one another, and are no longer manufactured.

Both weapons fire from a split trail platform on a two-wheel carriage and are crew-served by five to six men. The PAK 50 weighs 631kg and can fire HEAT rounds out to 600m range, whilst the PAK 57 is 716kg in weight and can engage targets with HEAT rounds out to 800m. Both weapons have gun shields fitted to provide the crew with some degree of protection against the effects of shell splinters and small arms fire.

The PAK 50 has a shield with a slight forward curve on the lower edge and is fitted with a muzzle brake. The PAK 57 has a more pronounced gun shield which is concave in shape towards the breech mechanism, but has no muzzle brake. Both weapons are credited with being capable of firing between eight and ten rounds per minute. More practical rates of fire would be observed when engaging moving targets.

These anti-tank guns are usually towed, but as Switzerland operates at least 15 Super Puma heli-copters, these could be used to rapidly airlift the guns around the battlefield.

	PAK 50	PAK 57
Calibre:	90mm	90mm
Overall weight:	641kg	716kg
Weight of shell:	1.95kg	2.7kg
Practical range:	300m	300m
Maximum range:	600m	800m
Muzzle velocity:	600m/sec	600m/sec

The PAK 50 has basic overall characteristics to distinguish it from the PAK 57, such as shape of gun field.

The PAK 57 is identified from the PAK 50 by its curved gun shield.

U.K.

The Swingfire is the heavyweight long-range anti-tank guided weapon of the British Army and as such has to be platform mounted on a specially adapted vehicle for firing. Swingfire entered service with the British Army in 1969, but its origins can be traced back even further. Until the introduction of Milan the Swingfire was the British Army's most modern, hard hitting anti-tank system in service, having replaced the older Vigilant. The Swingfire is canister-fired and is capable of being mounted for use from a wide range of vehicles, including Land Rovers. A trial to develop the missile into a helicopter launched system, to be known as Beeswing, was never pursued because TOW was taken into service for this purpose. The British Army currently uses a version of its FV432 APC to carry the Swingfire, which it launches from roof-mounted launcher bins. This is known as the FV438, and can carry a total of 14 Swingfire missiles. There are two launchers on the roof of the vehicle with the remaining 12 reload missiles carried internally. The launcher bins of the FV438 can be

reloaded from within the vehicle and guidance by means of MCLOS can also be performed from within the vehicle. However, should it be necessary there is the option to fire the Swingfire remotely. In this mode the operator leaves the vehicle and uncoils up to 100m of control cable away from the carrier vehicle. He can then connect it to his control unit sited in a concealed position. This method of operation would most likely be used where the operator can sight onto a target but moving the vehicle into a firing position might compromise the vehicle and invite counter-fire from the enemy. The Swingfire is rather stubby in appearance and weighs 37kg and carries a HEAT warhead capable of defeating most MBTs. The missile is 1.067m in length and 170mm in diameter with a span of 373mm over its cruciform wings. The solid fuel motor of the Swingfire will propel it to a range of 4000m, but the minimum engagement range is 150m. The second specialised vehicle to carry Swingfire is the FV102 Striker in the Scorpion range of Combat Vehicles Reconnaissance (Tracked) CVR(T)s.

Each vehicle of this type carries ten Swingfire missiles, five of which are ready to fire from a quintuple mount on the roof of the vehicle. However, unlike the FV438, the crew of this particular vehicle cannot reload the launcher bins from inside the vehicle with the five reload missiles. The launcher bins on both vehicles are raised for firing and lowered when not in use and can be traversed through a limited arc. The Swingfire is pre-programmed to fly into the centre of the line of sight within the operator's sight unit. He then guides it manually using a small joystick control. In-flight course corrections are usually only minor alterations, but there is provision to swing the missile through a course correction of up to 45 degrees in required. The Striker carrier vehicle is currently deployed at troop level of four vehicles in each of the three reconnaissance squadrons of an armoured reconnaissance regiment within the British Army. This gives each unit 40 missiles for engaging targets. At present there are some 120 FV102 Strikers in service with the British Army. The missile can be operated in a wide range of temperatures and terrains ranging from sub-zero to desert conditions. It is understood that 60 Striker vehicles have recently undergone a Swingfire Improved Guidance (SWIG) programme. This has replaced the old Swingfire equipment with digitally based technology to upgrade the systems 24 hour, all weather combat capability. For an old system design the Swingfire missile is still good for a few years yet, and may even stay in service long enough to augment the TRIGAT series when it begins to enter service by the end of the decade.

Body diameter:	170mm
Span:	373mm
Weight:	37kg
Length:	1,067mm
Min/max range:	150m/4,000m

The free-flight LAW 94 anti-tank system was formerly known as the LAW 80. It was introduced into the British Army as a replacement for both the Carl Gustav 84mm and the much lighter LAW 66mm, both of which were used in the Falklands War in 1982. However, the complete replacement of these older systems by LAW 94 is some way off, as the British Army still has considerable stocks of both weapons.

The '94' in the LAW 94's name is a reference to its calibre rather than a date of service. It is intended for issue to infantry units serving in the armoured or mechanised battalion roles, and is issued down to section levels when operating from APCs in the anti-tank role. This is a shoulder-fired, disposable weapon which has a flip out sight, in much the same manner as other similar anti-tank systems. The weapon can be used to engage targets out to ranges of 500m and has an in-built spotter rifle so the firer can gauge the distance more accurately than with just a simple optical sight. This contains five rounds of ballistically matched 9mm ammunition with a tracer element in the base to permit the firer to observe his fall of shot as it strikes the target. He can correct his aim if he observes his ranging shots falling too short or going over the target.

In combat the firer acquires his target through the weapon sights and quickly fires two or three spotting rounds of 9mm. When he is satisfied that they are striking the target he will then engage with the main projectile. This form of target ranging has been criticised, but despite this several other shoulder-fired anti-tank weapons use this form of spotting aid, and it is very common on larger RCLs in the 106mm and 120mm range. Whatever the critics say, spotter rifles have been proved to increase the first round hit probability of anti-tank weapons.

The shaped charge warhead of the projectile is 94mm in calibre and can defeat 650mm of armour. The weapon is carried by an infantryman in the folded mode which is one metre in length. This is quickly extended, and the protective end caps removed, into the firing mode which is 1.5m in length. A flip out sight allows the firer to acquire his target even in poor light conditions, and a special clip on night sight has also been developed.

The LAW 94 has been used as the basis for a series of remote fired weapons, which are proving popular. This range includes Addermine, Addermine/Arges and

John Norris

Adderlaze. The Addermine is a cradle-mounted system which is set off-route and initiated to attack a vehicle from the side when the sensor wire is tripped or broken by a passing vehicle. The Addermine/Arges is a fully autonomous off-route anti-tank system, again designed to attack the passing vehicle from the side at the optimum moment. Clip-on computer-controlled sensors can be programmed to enable the Addermine/Arges system to engage only specified types of vehicles. There is no point in wasting a powerful weapon such as this against a soft-skinned target, so only large, heavy targets, such as main battle tanks or MICVs, can be entered for engagement. Finally in the range is Adderlaze, which is another remotely fired weapon system using LAW94 as its weapon centre. By using coded laser pulses to fire the system, targets up to 2,000m distant can be engaged. It is possible to pre-site a series of these Adderlazes along a route known to be used by the enemy in order to break up their formation.

John Norris

Specifications for basic infantry LAW 94:

Total weight:	10kg
Overall length (carrying mode) :	1,000mm
Overall length (firing mode) :	1,500mm
Calibre of projectile:	94mm
Effective range:	500m
Rear danger area:	20m

The L6 Wombat 120mm recoilless weapon was developed as a replacement for the older British Army's Mobat, which was also an anti-tank RCL of 120mm calibre. The Wombat entered service in the 1960s, and soon after was taken into service by Australia. Despite being a hard hitting weapon it is now declared obsolete with the British Army, although it and certain other RCLs like it may be encountered elsewhere.

At one time the Wombat was to found wherever the British Army was deployed, from Belize to the Berlin Garrison and Hong Kong. In fact, the Berlin garrison was one of the last units of the British Army to have the Wombat on strength. Australia took a number of Wombats into service, but like Britain no longer has them in frontline service. Australian forces used some Wombats in limited action during their involvement in the Vietnam War, but they were not popular because of the fierce backblast.

Mounted on a two-wheeled carriage, from which it also fired, the Wombat had a full 360 degree traverse and could engage moving targets out to 750m and static targets out to 1,000m. A 12.7mm spotting rifle was mounted above the barrel to aid target engagement. The Wombat fired HESH anti-tank rounds which weighed 27.2kg, of which 12.84kg was the actual projectile, and could penetrate 400mm of armour. The backblast of the Wombat was fearsome and on firing likely to give one's position away to enemy spotters.

The Wombat could be mounted on a Land Rover 4x4 in the British Army, in 'portee' fashion, rather than towing it. This produced a low cost, but effective means of providing a reliable mobile anti-tank system, while at the same time reducing the wear and tear on the wheeled carriage. The Wombat was also fitted to the British Army's FV432 APC over the rear troop compartment, but in this role the vehicle never carried personnel. This particular version carried 14 rounds of HESH which was the standard anti-tank round for the Wombat. These vehicles were usually deployed at the rate of six to the support company of each Mechanised Infantry Battalion. However, this arrangement was never popular with the troops who found handling the long projectiles something of a problem on the FV432.

The Wombat could be man-handled over rough terrain to be sited in a well-prepared weapon pit from which it could fire in defensive roles.

Calibre:	120mm
Barrel length:	33.33 calibres
Rate of fire:	4rpm
Length:	3.86m
Width:	860mm
Height:	1.09m
Crew:	3

John Norris

Danny O'Neil

Danny O'Neil

UNITED STATES

One of the oldest designs of disposable, shoulder-fired anti-tank weapon systems is the 66mm M-72 Light Anti-armour Weapon. Commonly referred to as the LAW 66 and mostly associated with the US Army, it was designed and developed by an American company. The LAW 66 has a long service record, being heavily used in combat situations by several armies. It was widely used by US troops during the Vietnam War.

In the Falklands War of 1982, British troops used it extensively to destroy Argentinian positions that were well protected and well sited. As the war was drawing to a close, the British forces were advancing to Port Stanley. Men of A Company 3 Para reported that a French-designed Panhard AML 90 armoured car of the Argentinian Army was on the move. A man moved forward armed with a LAW 66 and destroyed the armoured vehicle with a single shot. There was no further activity by Argentinian armoured vehicles.

The LAW 66 is a lightweight weapon which can easily be carried by an infantryman by means of a sling, and it is compact enough to be useful to troops deploying from helicopters and APCs. Unfortunately advances in armoured technology have left the LAW 66 with little chance of being much use on the battlefield against modern MBTs. Today it would best be used against light wheeled vehicles or, as in the Falklands War, for destroying well dug-in positions.

The LAW 66 comes as a pre-loaded launch tube containing a HEAT rocket and can be handled with the utmost safety as a complete round of ammunition. The weight of 2.36kg means a man can carry two or three LAW 66s without any problem. The weapon is straightforward in design and use. On removing the safety pin the end plates drop down and the firer extends the telescopic launch tube to its firing length of 893mm. Basic 'pop up' sights are revealed, incremented in 25m stages out to 350m range. There is a safety handle, which prevents accidental discharge of the projectile and must be positively pushed forward. Then the firer simply places the tube on his shoulder, takes aim and depresses the firing mechanism on the top of the tube. This action releases the tension on the rod of the firing pin to allow it to strike the centre of the primer to fire the rocket.

The HEAT warhead of the rocket is typical point initiating base detonating (PIBD) in action, and will penetrate just over 300mm of armour. It would not cope against ERA but could be used to engage APCs. The rocket is fin stabilised and has an effective range of 150m against moving targets and 300m against stationary targets, but it will carry out to 1,000m if unchecked.

No longer in frontline service with many armies, the LAW 66 is still found in service with those forces who cannot or do not want to afford a replacement system. The LAW 66 is a useful anti-tank, or more correctly anti-vehicle, system which can add an extra force to assaulting infantry.

Calibre:	66mm
Overall weight:	2.36kg
Weight rocket:	1kg
Length closed:	655mm
Length extended:	893mm
Length of rocket:	508mm
Muzzle velocity:	145m/sec
Effective range:	150 to 300m
Armour penetration:	305mm

One of the more advanced methods of defeating and MBT is the Line Of Sight Anti-Tank (LOSAT) weapon system. This weapon is currently being developed by an American company. It does not use an explosive warhead, either HESH or HEAT, to destroy its target. Instead the LOSAT projectile is a Kinetic Energy Missile, KEM, which is designed to defeat the tank by means of kinetic energy alone. Because of this it has to be platform mounted, and a modified M3 Bradley is being used for trials purposes.

The KEM will feature all those on-board systems normally associated with anti-tank missiles, such as guidance processors, attitude control motors and roll reference sensors. The carrier vehicle mounts a retractable firing platform with at least four missiles ready to fire in a layout similar to the French army's Mephisto system. The American LOSAT system is designed to allow a crew of three men to engage MBT targets out ranges of 3,000m in only a few seconds. All commands, missile guidance and target acquisition, are by means of Forward Looking Infra-Red sensors mounted on the launch platform, and can be conducted under protection of the vehicle's armoured hull. Reloading the launching platform is also conducted from within the confines of the carrier vehicle.

The KEM missile travels at hypervelocity speeds, in excess of 1,500m/sec, and has been shown to be capable of defeating a target out to 3,000m. The KEM is 2,845mm in length, weighs 77kg and is 162mm in diameter. Because the system relies on kinetic energy to defeat the target the missile carries a long rod penetrator, which is a munition design normally associated with conventional ammunition fired from the main armament of an MBT. The long rod penetrator can be forged from either tungsten or depleted uranium, both of which are extremely dense alloys.

Impact from the missile on the target would carry spall, high velocity shrapnel from the armour and long rod penetrator, into the interior of the vehicle to disable it by smashing equipment and killing the crew. Due to the KEM's high closing speed it would be immune to ERA fitted to MBTs, because the missile would have penetrated into the vehicle's interior before the ERA could activate.

It is understood that once LOSAT has completed full firing trials, plans are in hand to reduce the overall length of the KEM to allow it to be fitted to a wide range of AFVs serving as carrier platforms. It could also be mounted on helicopters.

U.S. ARMY/ROCKWELL HELLFIRE
MODULAR MISSILE
DUAL WARHEAD CONFIGURATION

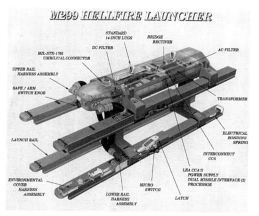

M299 HELLFIRE LAUNCHER

Starting life as an air-launched anti-armour weapon, the Hellfire missile has been developed into one of the most comprehensive weapon systems in the world. The American-developed Hellfire is most immediately associated with the AH-64 Apache attack helicopter, which can carry a payload of 16 Hellfire missiles in a weapon mix which can also include cannons.

However, Hellfire can be configured to many types of aircraft, including rotary and fixed-wing, ranging in size from the German Army's small BO105 helicopter through to the larger types such as the British Army's Lynx and the US Marine Corps' AH-1W Super Cobra. The Hellfire missile is capable of arming ground attack aircraft such as the OV-10 Bronco, AV-8B Harrier and A-10 Tankbuster. Fighter aircraft such as the F-16 and F/A-18 can also carry the Hellfire and the C-130 Hercules 'Spectre' Gun Ship has also been studied as a launch platform for the missile.

Although it is primarily regarded as an anti-tank missile the Hellfire has been trialled in launches from a Chaparral anti-aircraft vehicle turret, and shown to be capable of intercepting a drone helicopter target. There is even a naval version of this versatile system which can be sited to protect harbours and coastlines. However, it is in the anti-tank role that Hellfire really comes into its own, with some 18,000 missiles successfully deployed with American Coalition Forces during the 1991 war against Iraq in Desert Storm.

The Hellfire missile can be fitted to a wide range of military vehicles such as the 'HUMMER', which carries two missiles ready to launch on special rails fitted to a pedestal launcher mounted on the roof of the vehicle. The US Army's M-113 APC carries two launcher containers, each holding four missiles, to give eight Hellfire missiles ready to fire, with reload missiles carried internally. Even light strike vehicles such as the Saker and the Longline can carry a pair of Hellfire missiles ready to fire from basic launching rails. The HUMMER version weighs 1,500 (US) pounds and features a twin rail launcher and the fire control unit. There is enough space for the vehicle to carry eight reload missiles internally. The US Army's M3 Bradley APC has been trialled as a carrier for the Hellfire, also.

However, it is the helicopter with which the Hellfire system is most associated and the Apache attack helicopter can carry four special M299 quadruple launchers to give a weapon payload of 16 missiles. There are actually several types of Hellfire missile, but all use either IR or radio frequency IR seekers to home in on their target which has been illuminated by a target designating laser beam. The current range of missiles have semi-active laser seekers but millimetric wave and RF/IR seekers have been successfully trialled.

The Hellfire missile achieves pinpoint accuracy by homing in on reflected laser energy aimed at the target from either the launching helicopter, an escorting helicopter or even a ground-based forward observer. The Hellfire seeker is hardened against electro-optical countermeasures and contains an autopilot. It has been shown to be capable of flying to its target in all weather conditions and terrain.

The warhead is more normally the hollow-charge anti-tank type, but others are available including a special blast/fragmentation warhead. The Hellfire anti-tank warhead features a dual charge using a pre-cursor followed by a more powerful HEAT charge. In other words it is laid out along the tandem warhead design to defeat appliqué armour, ERA and other composite materials.

The Hellfire is devastating and can be fired from the launching platform in either single target engagement or in ripple fire to engage multiple targets. Apart from the current range of anti-tank systems, the Hellfire is being developed into more automated series. Future growth of the missile system allows for increased range and insensitive munitions. A single rail launcher has also been developed whereby the operator can use the missile from a tripod, but this would be used from well-prepared defensive positions because of the system's heavy weight – over 40kg for the tripod alone.

WEIGHT	LENGTH	SPEED
Laser A, B, C Models: 45.70kg	1.625m	Supersonic
Laser F Models: 48.60kg	1.803m	Supersonic
RF/IR: 47.88kg	1.727m	Supersonic
IIR: 47.88kg	1.778m	Supersonic

The American-built Tube-launched, Optically-tracked, Wire-guided anti-tank missile, TOW, is a widely used and widely copied system. Indeed it is the essential SACLOS guided system, which means all the operator has to do is maintain the target on the graticule lines in his sight unit. Built-in computers located within the body of missile respond to course corrections by means of the wire link. The TOW is not a small system and even though it can be fired from a tripod mount, it is more usually associated with being a platform-mounted anti-tank system.

The design of TOW began in 1962, but it was not until 1970 that it entered operational service with the US Army. Since that time it has been adopted into service by some 40 countries and used extensively in combat, particularly in the fierce Middle East wars. After being in service for more than twenty years it is only natural that TOW should undergo mid-life improvements, and these programmes have succeeded in maintaining TOW's lethality against all types of main battle tanks, even those fitted with explosive reactive armour (ERA).

One of the improvement programmes resulted in the development of the missile BGM-71C Improved TOW, which carries a 127mm diameter HEAT warhead that incorporates a telescopic stand-off probe to increase lethality. This was followed by the BGM-71D TOW-2 missile which features a HEAT warhead of 152mm diameter, again with the telescopic stand-off nose probe,

and capable of defeating 800mm of armour. This may seem like overkill, but is necessary to defeat modern composite armour and reactive armour types.

The tripod mounted version of TOW consists of six units: the tripod, traversing unit, launch tube, optical sight, and missile guidance and battery test equipment. The launch tube is a pre-loaded assembly that is fitted to the system as a complete round and replaced after firing. If required, the gunner/operator can use the built-in self-test facility to check the missile's state of readiness. The current range of fin-stabilised TOW missiles can be used to engage targets between 100m and 3,750m.

The TOW system has been adapted for firing from a wide range of vehicles, both armoured and light wheeled vehicles, in 'shoot and scoot' tactics. Several types of helicopters, including the British Army's Lynx, Italian Mangusta and the US Army's AH-64 Apache, can all be configured to carry up to eight TOW missiles in their weapon mix. The method of mounting the operator's sight guidance unit depends on the type of helicopter carrying the missile. For example on the AH-64 Apache the sight units are mounted in a turret on the nose of the aircraft and can be rotated through 120 degrees in azimuth and elevated between -60 degrees and + 30 degrees. In the Lynx and Mangusta the operator's sight unit can be either mast mounted or set in the roof of the cockpit. In the mast-mounted version, the sight allows the helicopter to remain hidden from view just that bit more when engaged in anti-tank roles across the battlefield.

The maximum target engagement remains unaltered and after the missile has hit the target a special device severs the trailing wires from the missile to prevent snagging. With the SACLOS guidance system in anti-tank helicopters, if the TOW operator can see the target he can engage it without deviating, even if it is off to one side off the aircraft's flight path.

The range of vehicles to which TOW can be fitted is extensive and includes AFVs and light wheeled vehicles. Some of the US Army's M113 APCs have been converted to carry the TOW on special elevating launch platforms. Designated as the M901 Improved TOW Vehicle, this features a special elevating platform with a pair of TOW missiles ready to fire. The missiles are fired and guided by the operator from under cover of the vehicle. The interior of the converted M113 APC allows for a number of reload missiles to be carried.

The other armoured vehicle of the US Army which carries the TOW in special launchers is the M2 /3 Bradley Infantry Fighting Vehicle. This APC carries the TOW launchers fitted to the side of its turret, armed with a 25mm cannon with a 7.62mm machine gun co-axially mounted. The interior of the vehicle is not given over entirely to carrying reload missiles, and an infantry combat section/squad of seven men can be carried into battle in addition to the three man crew operating the M2/3 Bradley. In this configuration the vehicle can carry two TOW missiles ready to fire with seven reload missiles carried internally, with little or no degradation to its primary battlefield role which is to serve as an APC and provide supporting fire as they move forward. In fact, the vehicle armed in this way will provide an infantry group with such comprehensive fire support that most obstacles will be suppressed.

The US Army's High Mobility Multi-purpose Wheeled Vehicle, commonly referred to as either the 'HUMMER' or 'HUMVEE', has also been configured to carry the TOW anti-tank missile launcher, in which role it can carry several reload missiles. Wheeled vehicles in the 4x4 range in service with the South Korean and Japanese Armies also carry TOW launchers.

Specifications for the BGM-71D TOW-2 Missile:

Length:	1,714mm
Span over stabilising fins:	343mm
Range:	65m to 3,750m
Weight of warhead:	5.9kg HEAT
Weight of basic launcher:	93kg
Weight of missile:	28.1kg
Armour penetration:	800mm

The Shoulder-launched Multi-purpose Assault Weapon, SMAW, is a lightweight, shoulder-fired infantry weapon system which has been developed specifically for the US Marine Corps. The SMAW is a versatile, lethal weapon system which can defeat battle tanks as well as fortified positions. The weapon allows the operator to engage targets whilst remaining in a protective position, greatly increasing his battlefield survival.

The weapon comprises of two main components: a reusable firing mechanism and a pre-loaded launch tube. Depending on the type of target he is going to engage, the firer selects either the HEDP tube or HEAA for attacking armoured vehicles, and inserts a magazine of ballistically matched spotting rounds to bring the target exactly into his sights. He quickly fires two or three rounds in much the same manner as the British Army's LAW 94. Once he is satisfied as to his accuracy and the target's range and point of strike, the operator will fire the main projectile.

The SMAW has a unique fusing and warhead design that gives a high probability of destroying the target first time. For example, the HEDP projectile has a fuse that is sensitive enough to detect the difference between a relatively soft target, such as a sand-bagged position, and a harder target, protected by concrete. On hitting the surface the fuse will calculate the optimum moment to initiate detonation of the warhead to produce the maximum effect behind the surface. The SMAW has a 96% reliability and will detonate behind concrete or timber with maximum effect.

The HEAA projectile will defeat main battle tanks, even up to an obliquity of 70 degrees at 500m range. However, SMAW does not carry a tandem charge HEAT warhead, so an MBT fitted with ERA may be outside its capability. It has been said that SMAW is one of the most powerful anti-tank weapons in its range. That is as maybe, but its usefulness to an infantryman with its dual purpose role cannot be argued with.

Weight ready to fire:	13.13kg HEDP, 13.96kg HEAA
Length ready to fire:	1,372mm HEDP, 1,372mm HEAA
Weight of firing mechanism:	7.5kg
Length of firing mechanism:	825mm
Weight of HEDP round:	5.95kg
Length of HEDP round:	749mm (encased)
Weight of HEAA round:	6.4kg
Length of HEAA round:	843mm (encased)

The AT8 is a version of the AT4, an anti-tank weapon currently in use by several countries. The AT8 combines the AT4's launch tube and propulsion system with the warhead of the US Marine Corps' Shoulder-launched Multi-purpose Assault Weapon, SMAW. Both the AT4 and SMAW were combat proven during Operation Just Cause and Operation Desert Storm by the US Marine Corps in the 1991 Gulf War against Iraq. Because weapons on which the AT8 is based are a proven combination, no protracted development programme is necessary.

Although classified as a 'bunker buster' capable of penetrating more than 200mm of concrete, the AT8 can be used to engage and defeat light AFVs such as APCs. When used against soft-targets such as sand-bagged positions, the projectile will bury itself into it and detonate at the optimum moment for maximum effect. Carrying over 1kg of explosive in its warhead the AT8 will defeat light wheeled vehicles and be useful in fighting in built up areas. Such dual-purpose weapons, like this and the SMAW, give the infantryman a much needed 'extra punch' on the battlefield and allow him to respond accordingly to the situation as it develops. The AT-8 can be targeted against a machine gun emplacement, but if a vehicle appears the firer can switch to engage this target instead.

Weight:	7.3kg
Length:	1,000mm
Calibre:	84mm
Muzzle velocity:	219m/sec
Effective range:	250m

The M18A1 RCL 57mm as used by the South Korean Army.

useful in either breaking up an infantry assault or disrupting a vehicle convoy, which it could do at its maximum range of engagement.

Calibre:	57mm
Overall weight of launcher:	25kg
Weight of tripod and sight:	22.5kg
Overall length:	1,564mm
Range:	450m to 1200m
Muzzle velocity:	365m/sec

The South Korean Army is listed as one of the last operators of this US-designed weapon which was declared obsolete a number of years ago. The M18A1 is a standard RCL weapon with an interrupted lug breech block operating with a percussion firing mechanism. Despite its age the weapon is capable of firing HEAT, HE and white phosphorous ammunition out to considerable ranges.

For engaging heavier AFVs the range of the M18A1 RCL is limited to 450m. However the WP smoke ammunition can be fired out to 3,976m for covering the movement of troops and vehicles or pinpointing targets for engagement by either mortars or artillery.

The weapon can be mounted on a light wheeled vehicle that would also transport the crew and a number of rounds ready to fire, or it can be fired from prepared positions using a tripod mount where it is served by a crew of two men. The complete weapon with tripod and sight is some 47.5kg in weight, but this can be broken down into manageable parts for manhandling by infantry.

Its usefulness against modern armoured vehicles would be in question, but when used against light wheeled vehicles or infantry in the open it would still be

Development of the M-47 'Dragon' system was started way back in 1964, but it was not until 1970 that full production could begin following a multi-year procurement programme for the US Army. Following that tender the original Dragon system was manufactured for several years, during which time it was taken up by a number of overseas countries. Since then Dragon has undergone mid-service life improvements so that today it is Dragon Generation III. It remains a single-man operated system using SACLOS guidance that can engage targets out to 1,500m.

The warhead operates on the shaped charge principle, and has been improved to take into account new generations of MBTs entering service. The sustainer motor has also been upgraded to give the missile flight times of 6.26 seconds to a range of 1,000m and 8.6 seconds to a range of 1,500m.

The Dragon is a shoulder-fired disposable system, with the Day/Night Tracker, DNT, being the only reusable part of the weapon. This newly developed clip-on unit allows the operator to track his target electronically to maximise missile strike whilst reducing operator induced errors. The DNT also features IR sensors to provide target acquisition out to 2,000m and full recognition at the optimum 1,500m engagement range.

The launcher-tube comes with an extendible bipod attached to the front end to permit the operator to gain a point of balance, particularly when tracking a moving target. The Dragon can be operated at temperatures between -25 degrees and +145 degrees, which makes it capable of being deployed with Rapid Deployment Forces and other special forces units, who may operate in such dramatic changes in temperatures.

The DNT will provide the operator with a 4.8 degree field of view during the day and 3.6 degree field of view at night. It has a battery life of four hours continuous operation which is more than sufficient for several uses with different launch tubes. The SACLOS guidance system is reliable and virtually interference-free, which increases the Dragon's first round hit capability. However, all this technology does not come free of charge and, with a complete system weight of 22.5kg, the Dragon is quite a bulky load for an infantryman to carry. The HEAT warhead has been greatly improved and the exact capabilities are still classified, but is known to have exceeded the performance of comparable medium anti-

The improved M-47 Dragon with day/night tracker.

Improved Dragon round.

tank systems in current service.

The M-47 Dragon is an anti-tank weapon fully dedicated to use by infantrymen and has not been adapted for use from AFV or helicopter mountings. Its limited engagement range does not make it suitable for such applications where the preferred missiles have a range of at least 2,000m and preferably longer, as with HOT and TOW.

Length of launcher tube:	1154mm
Weight of launcher tube:	15.6kg
Weight of DNT:	6.9kg
Minimum engagement range:	65m
Maximum engagement range:	1500m

Original M-47 Dragon ATGW.

M-47 Dragon as it was deployed in the 1970s and 1980s.

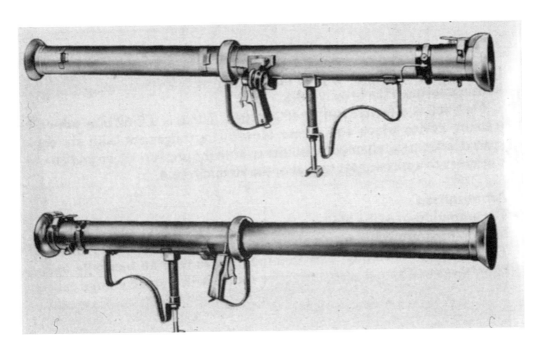

This US-designed weapon is no longer in service with the US Army. Some sources classify it as obsolete, but the M-20 is still in service with several countries, including South Korea. China even manufactured a copy of this weapon as the 90mm Type 51 anti-tank rocket launcher, and sold it to overseas client states. The M-20 was in service in time to be used during the Korean War, but developments in AFV designs soon relegated it to second line status.

Sometimes referred to as the 'Super Bazooka', the M-20 fires an electrically initiated rocket of 89mm calibre out to 1,200m maximum range, although 110m is more practical for the engagement of armoured targets. The M-20 is a two-piece weapon served by a two-man crew, one to aim and fire with the second man to load. With no moving parts to replace or maintain, the M-20 is unlikely to wear out under normal conditions and only severe damage would write one off.

More modern, lightweight weapons are available, but current users of the M-20 are unlikely to replace those they have in service, no doubt preferring to wait until it is absolutely necessary to purchase replacement weapons.

This is a familiar approach to replacing anti-tank weaponry with modern missiles or disposable systems. The policy appears to be 'if it works and there is a suitable supply of ammunition, leave it in service'. This approach is fine until one goes to war, when old-style weapons can severely hamper the troops' operational capability.

Calibre:	89mm (3.5 inch)
Length of launcher:	1,549mm (assembled)
Weight of launcher:	5.5kg
Range:	110m to 1,200m
Armour penetration:	267mm
Muzzle velocity:	98m/sec

The M40A2 RCL is basically a continuation of the widely used and highly popular M40 RCL series. The M40A2 is of the same calibre, that is to say 106mm and fires HEAT and HEP-T, high explosive practice-tracer, but this last type of ammunition is used for training purposes. The small army of Cameroon still holds at least 40 RCLs of the type M40A2 and makes it one of the last users of this type of weapon. The weapon can either be towed on a two-wheeled carriage, but is more popularly mounted on a fixing for direct firing from a 4X4 wheeled vehicle. The M40A2 fires its HEAT round at 308m per second out to a maximum range of 2745m, but the practical anti-tank range is just over 1000m range. The weapon can traverse a full 360 degrees and elevate between -17 degrees and +65 degrees and achieve the realistic rate of fire of one round per minute. It is crewed by two to four men and the M40A2 features the standard 12.7mm spotting rifle to aid ranging on to targets. It weighs 220kg in its travelling mode which makes it light enough to be manhandled over rough terrain if necessary.

Calibre:	106mm.
Barrel length:	26.8 calibres:=2.840m
Length overall:	3.4m.
Range maximum:	2745m (HEAT)
Crew:	2-4.
Weight:	220kg.
Muzzle velocity:	308m per second.

South Korean Army firing the M40A2 RCL.

FORMER YUGOSLAVIA

The M57 anti-tank launcher, in service with various forces in the former Yugoslavia, is very old-fashioned in appearance. However, the projectile with its oversized warhead of 90mm is still quite powerful and will penetrate 300mm of armour. This makes it useful against older types of MBTs and most APCs.

The weapon consists of a reusable launch tube which is shoulder-fired like the RPG-2 and RPG-7 in principle. The M57 has a permanently fitted bipod for aiding stability during aiming and tracking a moving target. It is served by a two-man crew who act as firer and loader. Like the RPG-2 and RPG-7 this weapon has an oversized warhead which means it has to be loaded through the muzzle of the launch tube. The launcher incorporates optical sights and has a firing pin mechanism to actuate the propellant charge of the fin-stabilised HEAT projectile. It is compact enough to equip troops operating from APCs or helicopters.

Diameter of launch tube:	44mm
Calibre of projectile:	90mm
Length of launcher:	960mm
Weight of launcher:	8.2kg
Weight of projectile:	2.4kg
Maximum range:	200m
Penetration:	300mm

The M60 crew-served RCL weapon is in service with various forces in the former Yugoslavia. It was designed and developed locally for the Yugoslavian Army before the break up of the country. It is a light weapon for its size and can be manhandled over rough terrain into defensive positions, but it is more usually towed behind light wheeled vehicles. The locally produced fin-stabilised HEAT rounds can be used to engage moving targets out to 1,000m and stationary targets out to 1,500m, and will penetrate 220mm of armour at 500m range.

The M60 is mounted on a compact two-wheeled carriage from which it is also fired. This permits a full 360 degree traverse and elevation between -20 degrees and +35 degrees, to make it extremely versatile in mountainous terrain. The crew of five can put down a rate of fire of around four to five rounds per minute if necessary. The weapon can be operated by only two men in an emergency if required, but in this instance the rate of fire would probably drop to two or three rounds per minute.

The HEAT rounds for the M60 weigh 7.2kg and will carry out to nearly 4,000m range. The M60 can also fire HE rounds in the indirect fire role, and these have a range of 4,500m but accuracy at this range would not be good. This role would be reserved for harassing fire of infantry or soft-skinned light wheeled vehicles.

Calibre:	82mm
Overall length:	2.2m
Weight:	122kg
Muzzle velocity:	388m/sec
Range (HEAT):	1,000m moving target,
	1,500m stationary target
Penetration:	220mm

This is the replacement weapon of the standard US 105mm RCL M-65 and was developed in the former Yugoslavia. Despite its old-fashioned appearance, reliable sources claim that at least 650 of these weapons are currently in use with Serbia-Montenegran forces. It is a rifled weapon which is crew-served and can be towed on its two-wheeled carriage or mounted directly on light vehicles for battlefield mobility.

For target engagement the M-65 uses a UB 12.7mm spotting rifle mounted on top of the barrel. This is fed from a 20 round belt, which can fire either single rounds or automatic, and allows the crew to engage targets at ranges between 100m and 600m. It can fire both HEAT and HE ammunition, the latter out to 6,000m maximum for engaging soft targets such as infantry and wheeled vehicles where accuracy is not so important and the intention is more to harass and break up a formation as it moves across open country.

The HEAT round can be used against vehicles out to ranges between 100m and 600m and will penetrate 330mm of armour, which is a useful level of lethality but unlikely to cause any serious damage to a modern MBT.

Calibre:	105mm
Overall length:	4.55m
Width travel position:	1.43m
Height travel position:	1.14m
Weight in firing position:	280kg
Rate of fire:	six rounds per minute
Range:	HEAT 600m maximum, HE 6,000m maximum practical

INTERNATIONAL

To complement the TRIGAT Long Range system the medium range TRIGAT is being developed to replace infantry systems currently nearing their end of service life. These systems include Milan and the American-built Dragon, both of which have undergone mid-service upgrades to maintain their effectiveness against modern main battle tanks which are appearing with reactive armour protection. The Medium Range TRIGAT is being developed by the same consortium as the Long Range TRIGAT, that is to say the Euromissile Dynamics Group, which has input from Britain, France and Germany. The Medium Range TRIGAT will comprise a pre-loaded launch tube, weighing around 16kg, and be fired from a firing post weighing some20kg, which is not dissimilar in layout to the current Milan system. The MR TRIGAT will capable of being fitted to vehicles or man-portable and have a target engagement range between 200m and 2000m. The time of flight for the missile out to the maximum 2000m range will be around twelve seconds. As with the Long Range TRIGAT the exact details of this system are still very guarded, but it is understood the guidance system will be laser beam-riding. This system is proof against countermeasures and all the firer has to do is simply keep his target in sight on the graticule lines and the missile's built-in computer will respond to the coded laser illumination signals, originating from either the launching post or a secondary source, to home in on both stationary and moving targets. The Medium Range TRIGAT will have a tandem warhead charge also, which will allow it to defeat vehicles fitted with reactive armour. The tandem charge principle is simply a small shaped or hollow charge mounted in front of a much larger, more powerful charge. The first charge will blast the reactive armour to allow the larger warhead to penetrate the armour of the vehicle proper. A passive IRCCD, known as 'Tiger' night vision unit is being developed and will be introduced along with the missile to allow all-weather, 24 hours a day operation of Medium Range TRIGAT. The system has been shown to work well, but with an estimated cost of some £25,000,000 per missile this might prove prohibitive to some countries who might be considering purchasing this weapon as a replacement for their Milan missiles.

The MR TRIGAT is being developed for use in built-up areas which will allow it to be used from within confined spaces. This is made possible through a specially developed 'soft launch' technique that eliminates backblast. After launch a thrust-vector motor takes over to propel the missile to its target. It has a fast time into action and will allow up to three missiles per minute to be launched. The MR TRIGAT has been developed to have nuclear hardening to allow continued functioning under even the most hostile conditions on the battlefield. At present the Medium Range TRIGAT has an in-service date set for 1998 or 1999, but the inevitable spiralling costs that come with such developments might cause some delays.

The long-range TRIGAT system is designed to replace the older, now ageing anti-tank missiles with ranges of 4000m. It is at present still in the final stages of development, but already proves itself capable of engaging and destroying targets at ranges from 500m to 8000m. TRIGAT will be a platform-mounted weapon, as its overall combat weight will prevent it from being carried by an infantryman and it must therefore be mounted on either a special tank-hunting helicopter or a vehicle. It will be provided with an all-round, all-weather capability to give it a 24 hour anti-tank role on the battlefield. Using the advance Automatic Command to Line Of Sight, ACLOS, the TRIGAT will, nevertheless, be easy to operate from either helicopters or vehicles. With a 'lock on before launch' capability a high level of first round first hits is ensured. The exact details of the warhead are still classified, but it is known to be of a highly advanced design with a fire and forget programme feature, using a tandem charge to penetrate spaced armour and reactive armour and destroy all future predicted main battle tank designs. The sighting system of TRIGAT will be multi-channel capable of using IR CCD, infra-red charge-coupled devices and TV, which are both passive systems, to track the missile to its target. A typical helicopter mounting for TRIGAT would consist of a single pod, each containing four missiles, mounted either side of the fuselage to give a total of eight missiles. In this role the sight, known as 'OSIRIS', would be mast-mounted above the rotor blades to allow the helicopter to loiter behind natural obstacles, such as woodland, to avoid being observed. Such a deployment allows the helicopter gunner/firer to make his assessment of the target very quickly; such as recognition, terrain and range to target. Once selected he can fire either a single TRIGAT or up to four missiles to engage four separate targets. Such is the speed of the TRIGAT system that an operator can engage four targets with four missiles in under eight seconds. The vehicle-mounted version of TRIGAT would operate in a similar way, possibly using a telescopic mast to mount the stabilised sight. The TRIGAT programme is designed to replace anti-tank missiles currently used in the platform mounted role, such as the American-designed

TOW and the Milan, both of which have undergone mid-life improvements to maintain their lethality against modern armour protection such as add-on reactive armour. Originally designed to complement the multi-national European-designed Tiger helicopter, which has not been selected by Britain, there is no reason why TRIGAT could not be applied to other helicopters, such as the Italian Mangusta or American AH-64 Apache. Indeed, France and Germany are still committed to purchasing the Tiger helicopter for anti-tank duties and will, no doubt, be fitting the TRIGAT system to this platform to provide their respective armed forces with a missile of all-round capability which is proving to be highly efficient in its given role of tank killer. The Long-Range TRIGAT system features a Defensive Aids Suite, DAS, to make it resistant to countermeasures of all types and improve its overall battlefield effect.

Since the Franco-German Milan anti-tank missile started to service in the mid-to-late 1970s it has been taken up by a number of countries and can only be rivalled by the US-designed TOW missile system in popularity. Milan is an acronym for 'MIssile Leger ANti-char', translating into light anti-tank missile. Over the past few years it too has had to undergo improvements programmes to increase the lethality of its warhead to maintain pace with ERA and composite armours. The Milan can be deployed with infantry, requiring a three-man crew, vehicle mounted and helicopter mounted, thereby equalling TOW for variation in deployment configurations. Indeed the French, British and German Armies use Milan in all three applications. The missile is SACLOS guided and has been used extensively in a number of conflicts around the world. In 1982 during the Falklands War British troops used Milan missiles to destroy several Argentinian heavy machine gun positions, which were beyond the range of normal infantry weapons. The accuracy of the Milan in this role was greatly appreciated. In 1987 an incident between Chad and neighbouring Libya sparked off a brief but particularly violent clash of arms. Chad deployed 12 Milan anti-tank missile firing posts mounted on Toyota light trucks and these accounted for more than 60 Libyan tanks of the type T-55 and T-62 MBTs. The French, British and German Armies place great emphasis on Milan. With the British army the Fire Support Company of an Armoured Infantry Battalion would hold 24 Milan firing posts in three sections each with six posts, the remaining six firing posts being held by the mobilisation section. A total of 200 missiles would be available to them. In a Mechanised Infantry Battalion 24 Milan firing posts would be deployed equally to four sections in the specialised Milan Platoon of the Support Company. However, in the specialised 24 Airmobile Brigade, which serves primarily as a dedicated anti-tank unit, the two airmobile infantry battalions each hold 42 Milan firing posts to give a total of 84 units within the Brigade, with the associated number of Milan missiles. The British Army places such high regard on the Milan missile that it is believed to have purchased or ordered some 50,000 missiles to date. The Milan is a second generation anti-

tank guided missile using SACLOS and has an ongoing improvement programme to allow it to keep pace with developments in MBT protection, including ERA and other composite armours. The missile originated in France with technical support from German defence manufacturers, but it must now be classed a truly international weapon. The Milan is an all-weather 24 hours a day system due largely to the MIRA (TI) sight which can be mounted on the firing post. The Milan system comprises of only two components, the pre-loaded launch tube and the firing post that contains the guidance system for the missile's on-board computer to respond to the SACLOS signals. The missile is fired from

launch tube by means of a booster charge gas generator to impart an initial velocity of 75m/sec. When the missile is two or three metres out from point of launch, a two-stage propulsion motor ignites to burn for the full 12.5 seconds it takes for it to fly 2,000m to its maximum target engagement range. All the operator has to do is maintain the graticule lines of his sight unit on the target and the missile responds to his commands and hits the target. This is common with all SACLOS guided missiles. The Milan alters course by means of a jet spoiler and automatically adjusts to course corrections. On firing, the spent launch tube is ejected rearwards off the launching rail of the firing post, leaving it free for the second crewman to reload another launcher tube. The latest version is based on the Milan 2T and incorporates further resistance to countermeasures and has an extremely powerful warhead. However, these latest developments have led to a new firing post being developed, also, to accommodate it. The overall dimensions remain the same and the weight has only been increased marginally. The Milan can be fired from a wide range of vehicle both wheeled and tracked. The British Army have firing posts capable of being used from Land Rover 4X4 vehicles and their Milan Compact Turret allows for a retrofit to a CVR(T) in the Scorpion range of armoured vehicles. The French Army uses Milan from

the M11 light armoured wheeled reconnaissance vehicle and wheeled vehicles and the German Army has Milan adapted to fire from the Marder MICV. Milan can also be fired from various types of helicopter such as the Lynx, Gazelle and BO 105. These are all capable of carrying multiple loads of Milan and mount their tracking optical sight unit in either the roof of the cockpit or mast-mounted for full SACLOS control. When Milan is fired from a helicopter the launch tube does not eject from the launch rails, otherwise it could strike the tail rotor. There is also a special guillotine device which severs the control wire after the missile has hit the target. This prevents it from snagging the airframe of the helicopter and causing a hazard. The Milan will remain in service for some considerable time and not likely to be replaced entirely by the TRIGAT system when it begins to enter **131** service. The chances of a first round hit with Milan at a range of 250m is calculated at an average of 75%. At ranges of 2000m this increases to a 98% probability, due to the extra time gained by the longer flight time to the target, which allows adjustments to be made by the operator.

	M1	M2	M2T	M3
Weight in carrying mode:	12.23kg	12.23kg	12.62kg	12.62kg
Weight in firing mode:	11.52kg	11.52kg	11.91kg	11.91kg
Length in carrying mode:	1260mm	1260mm	1260mm	1260mm
Length in firing mode:	1200mm	1200mm	1200mm	1200mm
Diameter:	133mm	133mm	133mm	133mm
Missile:				
Weight:	6.73kg	6.73kg	7.12kg	7.12kg
Length:	769mm	918mm	918mm	918mm
			non-extended nose	non-extended nose
			1138mm extended nose	1138mm extended nose
Diameter, wings folded:	125mm	125mm	125mm	125mm
Wingspan:	267mm	267mm	267mm	267mm
Warhead:				
Weight:	2.67kg	2.70kg	3.12kg	3.12kg
Diameter:	103mm	115mm	117mm	117mm
Explosive filling:	1.36kg	1.79kg	1.83kg	1.83kg
Cone diameter:	101mm	112.9mm	112.9	112.9mm

Type of firing post:	MILAN			MILAN3
Munitions:	M1, M2, M2T			All munitions
Weight:	16.4kg			16.9kg
Length:	900mm			900mm
Height:	650mm			650mm
Width:	420mm			420mm

APPENDICES

The use of mortars may not seem appropriate for anti-tank roles, but recent developments in mortar projectile technology allow the upper surfaces of the engine decking and turret roof of an MBT to be successfully attacked. These surfaces on an MBT are by their very design left thinly armoured compared to the side and frontal surfaces, and are therefore easier to penetrate when attacked by anti-tank weapons. Apart from one missile system currently in service the upper surfaces of an MBT are very rarely attacked directly. However, the plunging effect of projectiles fired from mortars permit this form of attack against MBTs. Under normal circumstances mortar bombs with conventional HE filling would not affect a tank apart from possibly damaging the crew's vision blocks or other externally mounted optical systems. This short-coming has now been redressed due to developments in Britain and Sweden. The British anti-tank mortar round, known as Merlin, has a calibre of 81mm and can be fired from either the British Army's standard L16 mortar or the US Army's M252

mortar, which equip the support companies of normal infantry battalions. The British Merlin project was announced in June 1984 and has attracted considerably attention, but at the time of writing has still to enter service with any armed force. The Merlin system is a very advanced, fire and forget system, requiring little in the way of training. It is an autonomous projectile which detects an armoured vehicle during flight and guides itself onto the target to attack from above. During the initial phase of the Merlin's trajectory it flies ballistically as a normal mortar round and the warhead is armed and the electronics and seeker head engage. At the apogee of its trajectory, the Merlin's millimetric guidance sensor begins to search the ground around its impact area for a possible target. The forward canard fins deploy and the projectile begins to stabilise itself to a 45 degree angle, which develops into a 60 degree angle to dive on to the target – at which time velocity is some 140 metres per second. The sensor is sensitive enough to penetrate smoke and dust of the battlefield and comb a 300m²

Merlin is loaded like a standard mortar round. Despite ease of use it has not been purchased.

area. The first moving target sensed by the Merlin round will be tracked and engaged, even if it moves out of the original sensory pattern. Should the Merlin fail to detect a moving target it will seek likely stationary targets within a 100m² area. When a target is detected the Merlin will plunge onto the thinly armoured upper surface areas of the vehicle. It can be fired in salvoes of up to ten rounds per minute and used to break up armoured assaults. Trials have shown the Merlin to be a workable system, but it still remains un-used. It has a full all-weather capability and a reliability of better than 90% out to a maximum range of 4200m. The Swedish anti-tank mortar system is known as the Strix and is in the much larger calibre of 120mm. It too is launched in the conventional manner of a standard mortar round and has a maximum range of 8000m. The Strix carries a passive IR seeker and terminal guidance to make it a true fire and forget system, and like its smaller counterpart requires only a minimal amount of training. Because it uses IR seekers to detect its target, the Strix sensor homes in on the hot emissions from a vehicle's engine or exhaust. Terminal guidance toward the identified target, whether stationary or moving, is made by means of side thruster rockets to provide rapid trajectory corrections. The HEAT warhead of the Strix penetrates even ERA and has a behind armour effect in the form of overpressure, fragmentation, heat and blast to disable the vehicle. The range of the Strix can be altered by attaching special charges to a tail unit of the round in addition to the separate sustainer motor which is fitted after the tail unit for maximum target engagement ranges. Most 120mm mortars are of the towed variety which means that the prime mover vehicle can carry a supply of Strix rounds along with the crew. Vehicles thus equipped can be used as mobile mortar batteries to break up armoured assaults. These two types of anti-tank projectiles add a new dimension to attacking armour and will no doubt influence approaches to the problem of dealing with assaults by massed tanks and infantry assaulting in APCs.

	Merlin	Strix
Calibre:	81mm	120mm
Weight:	7kg	17kg
Length:	900mm	810mm
Range:	4200m	8000m
Seeker:	Millimetric	IR
Time of flight:	40 seconds	

The use of mines may appear to some people an unfair way to attack tanks and other armoured vehicles. But any means of making the enemy do something a defender wants must surely be rated as a success.

Anti-tank mines have been in widespread use since the Second World War and the idea behind their use on the modern battlefield is the same as it was more than fifty years ago. The intention is to channel the vehicles into well-prepared 'killing zones' which are heavily covered by well-sited anti-tank weapons.

Anti-tank mines attack their targets in two ways. They can attack from underneath, defeating the thin 'belly' armour or cutting the tracks. Or they can attack the vehicle from the side as it passes along a route.

Buried anti-tank mines are initiated by a direct pressure of between 200kg to 250kg, which means under normal circumstances a vehicle will detonate the device. During the Falklands War in 1982, the defending Argentinian forces laid thousands of mines, both anti-tank and anti-personnel. But even then the British forces lost only one light tank to anti-tank mine action. In the British Army the Bar Mine anti-tank mine is the preferred method of laying a defensive minefield. This is laid by means of a mechanical plough attached to a vehicle such as an FV 432. The plough exposes a shallow trench into which a mine is laid by means of a small conveyor belt. The earth is then replaced by means of a chain dragging the spoil back into place. This does not try to disguise the fact that activity has taken place, but does serve to alert the enemy to the fact that mines have been laid in a specific area. Either this will cause a delay in the enemy's advance as he tries to breach the minefield, or he will seek a way round the obstacle – in which case he may blunder into a prepared screen of anti-tank missiles laid out in advance for the specific purpose of attacking the armoured column in force.

The Bar Mine is 1.2m in length, 100mm in width and weighs 11kg, of which 8.4kg is the explosives content. The French Army uses a similar system and the Russian Army also has its version of ploughing in or burying anti-tank mines. Whatever the system, the result is the same – to channel the tank into a killing zone.

Horizontal action mines, such as the French-

designed device of the same name and in use with the British Army, have limitations, particularly against those vehicles carrying ERA.

Minefields are usually laid by an engineer unit who have the specialised equipment to perform such tasks. The laying of minefields is a labour-intensive, time-consuming task. For example 600 Bar mines can be laid in one hour by a three-man crew operating from an FV 432. But since such a vehicle is incapable of carrying such a payload several vehicles will be involved, along with the associated logistics and back-up.

Anti-tank mines are an efficient way of either breaking up or delaying armoured attacks, and provide the defender with much-needed time to organise his anti-tank defences even further and possibly call in anti-tank helicopters carrying long-range missiles.

During the Second World War a number of new tank designs emerged to exploit particular tactical situations as they arose. Some were so bizarre they defied the imagination, such as the Germans giant tank programme with the E100 and Maus projects. Other designs were variants on a theme and produced the workable airportable light tanks for transportation in gliders, such as the British Tetrarch and US M22 Locust. One design of AFV that emerged then and has left its mark on AFV designs was the tank destroyer.

Put simply, the tank destroyer was a well-armoured hull, usually on an existing and proven chassis, with a large calibre gun mounted in either a fully traversing turret or semi-fixed directly into the hull. The Germans were leaders in this AFV design, but the Allies did develop a handful of their own tank destroyer designs. The wartime tank destroyer design continued in service after the war and today there are still several dedicated tank destroyer designs in service around the world.

One could argue that the best method of destroying an MBT is to use another MBT, but logistically speaking the tank destroyer is a cost-effective option. All tank destroyer designs in service at present are of ageing designs and should be consigned to the reserve material lists, but they serve on despite their age and limited use on the battlefield.

In theory any AFV that carries an anti-tank weapon can be termed a tank destroyer, such as the British Army's Striker with Swingfire missiles or the German Army's Jaguar with HOT missiles, but they are not seen as such in classification terms. The Austrian Army still figures some 282 Jagdpanzer SK 105 Kurassier, which it terms as self-propelled anti-tank guns. These are listed separately from their other MBTs. Known more simply as the SK 105, the design programme of this Austrian vehicle was started in 1965, with the first prototypes appearing in 1967 and entering service with the Austrian Army proper in the early 1970s. Armed with a 105mm gun in a fully traversing, oscillating turret, capable of firing HEAT rounds, the SK 105 has been developed into other variants and sold to several overseas countries.

The German Army has the Jagdpanzer Kanone, which also has the Rakete (Rocket) version which carries the HOT missile and is known as the Jaguar. The Jagdpanzer Kanone, Jpz 3-4, entered service with the German Army in 1965 and just over 700 vehicles were built. The layout is similar to old wartime designs, with the 90mm gun mounted directly into the front of the hull with a traverse limited to 15 degrees left and right and elevation between -8 degrees and +15 degrees. The German Army still counts eight of these vehicles, classed as self-propelled anti-tank guns, as being in service.

The Japanese Ground Self Defence Force (Army) has over 200 vehicles of the Type 60 tank destroyer which features twin 106mm RCLs mounted on a tracked chassis to grant it the status of self-propelled anti-tank gun. Introduced into service in 1960 the Type 60 tank destroyer is used only by the JSDF. The two 106mm RCLs fire HEAT rounds for which ten reloads are carried, which does somewhat limit the length of time the vehicle could function for in combat. The twin 106m RCLs can traverse 10 degrees left and right and elevate between -5 degrees and +10 degrees in the low firing setting. In the upper or raised setting the RCLs traverse 30 degrees left and right and can be elevated from -20 degrees to +15 degrees.

The Russian Army lists two dedicated tank destroyers in its inventory of AFVs. First it has the ASU-57 which carries a 57mm gun capable of firing HVAP, APHE and HE rounds. Secondly it has the much heavier ASU-85 which mounts an 85mm gun capable of firing HVAP, HE and APHE rounds, also. Both vehicles are capable of being deployed in an airportable role and are therefore flexible in their battlefield application. The term ASU stands for 'Aviadezantnaya Samochodnaya Ustanovka', and literally means Airborne Assault Gun. The 57mm APHE and HVAP rounds of the ASU-57 will penetrate 85mm and 100mm of armour at 1,000m range respectively. The 85mm APHE and HVAP rounds of the ASU-85 will penetrate 102mm and 130mm of armour respectively at 1,100m range. From these figures it will be seen that they both have limitations as tank destroyers and engaging MBTs with ERA or other composite armour. One has to conclude, therefore, that the element of surprise when deployed in the airborne role, is the greatest advantage these vehicles have during an assault phase.

The Swedish Army has the Infanterikanonvagn 91, IKV-91, designated as tank destroyers and has 210 such vehicles listed along with other AFVs. Production of the IKV-91 started in 1974 and entered service with the Swedish Army in 1975. It mounts a 90mm low pressure gun in a fully traversing turret and can fire fin stabilised HEAT rounds. It is doubtful whether such tank destroyers would be deployed to serve in the specific role for which they are intended, because this would severely limit their combat status. It is more likely they would be deployed in conventional armoured roles and take advantage of targets of opportunity as they presented themselves.

The range of vehicles listed here as tank destroyers are not capable of firing either the American 'Shillelagh' or Russian AT-8 'Songster' missiles which are fired from the main armament guns of the M551 Sheridan and T-80 tanks respectively. This is because those vehicles listed as being dedicated Tank Destroyers are not capable of firing these missiles, which are both SACLOS guided. Instead these gun-armed Tank Destroyers use conventional shells.

	SK105	JPZ4-5	TYPE 60	ASU 57	ASU 85	IKV 91
Country	Austria	Germany	Japan	Russia	Russia	Sweden
Crew	3	4	3	3	4	4
Hoight	2.53m	2.085m	1.30m	1.10m	2.1m	2.355m
Length	5.58m	8.75m	4.3m	4.995m	6m	6.14m
Width	2.50m	2.98m	2.23m	2.086m	2.8m	3m
Weight	17500kg	27500kg	8000kg	3350kg	14000kg	15500kg
Speed	65.5kph	70kph	45kph	45kph	44kph	69kph
Range	520km	400km	130km	250km	260km	550km
Armament	105mm	90mm	2x106mm RCL	57mm	85mm	90mm
Armour		10-50mm	15mm	6mm	10-40mm	

The various systems covered in this book have been compiled in such a way as to present you, the reader, with an overview of the different anti-tank weapons currently in service with armies around the world. Some weapons will no doubt be familiar to you and will be relatively new. Some are obviously so old that it is a wonder they still find their way into service. The countries that still hold them either are in no financial position to up-grade, or they have no requirement at present to replace these old-fashioned systems. However, what of the future?

The conclusion one immediately draws is that the anti-tank weapon, in whatever form, is very firmly here to stay, either in free-flight rocket or guided missile form. Some future projects have been outlined in the main text, but the really futuristic systems are still in the planning stage. The shoulder-fired, disposable systems widely available to the infantry will no doubt become lighter and more compact, whilst at the same time becoming more powerful as explosives technology develops.

The heavier, long-range anti-tank systems will still remain platform-mounted affairs going along the lines of Lock-On-Before-Launch and Lock-On-After-Launch to be fully fire-and-forget ACLOS systems. Laser beam-riding will probably remain, too, in which case the system of trailing wires as with the current range of SACLOS missiles will be eradicated.

These future heavy-weight, long-range missiles will continue to be carried on dedicated anti-tank helicopters, but the vehicle mounted systems may well use elevating platforms to obtain, track and engage targets at all distances. These elevating platforms would allow the launching/carrier vehicle to remain screened behind an obstacle such as a building or concealed in a group of trees, to avoid being engaged by enemy fire. The elevating launching platform would contain all the necessary optronics for the crew in the vehicle to engage their target and launch the anti-tank missiles, which would presumably be fire and forget types. All that would be visible would be the launching pod, containing either six or eight missiles at the end of an elevating arm. This could be as compact as one cubic metre in size. The

operator would remain in the vehicle and observe the situation through a real-time link monitor mounted on the launching platform. This would also contain IR and thermal imaging units for full 24 hour capability. A built-in test equipment (BITE) programme would ensure operational readiness at all times.

Such systems have been investigated by several countries, including Britain, France and Germany. They have been trialled in some instances and shown to work. Trials have used the French HOT system, but TRIGAT could quite easily be used from such a platform. However

the full requirement for elevating anti-tank systems is not at present deemed to be a military necessity.

One must, therefore, conclude that anti-tank weapons are not set for any radical change, beyond developing long-range fire and forget missiles and increasing the lethality of shoulder-fired, disposable weapons. The HEAT and HESH warheads are still the best method of dealing with an MBT and will remain so for the foreseeable future. Which in turn means that the older weapons will still be around for some time to come.

The origins of the infantry weapon system known as rifle grenade can be traced back to the time just before the outbreak of the First World War in 1914. During that conflict the rifle grenade in its anti-personnel form was used extensively by both Allied and Central powers in all theatres where trench-warfare stalemate existed. The intervening years from 1918 to 1939 saw the rifle grenade being developed into anti-tank versions, such as the German Army's Panzer Granate and the US Army's M-9, for use against various types of AFVs. The effectiveness of these early anti-tank rifle grenades was governed by the level of armour protection carried by a vehicle, but were generally considered as being better than nothing at all.

The rifle grenade is either a device manufactured specifically for launching from the muzzle of a standard rifle, or is a carrier system which has been designed to use the basic hand grenade as a conversion kit.

Rifle grenades were at one time commonly fired by means of a ballistite cartridge being loaded in place of the normal ammunition, and which produced large volumes of propellant gases on firing. In effect, it was a very powerful blank round which imparted the forward motion to the grenade. The angle of the rifle on firing determined the range of the rifle grenade, which was never very far, but farther than a hand thrown grenade. This method of firing rifle grenades has now given way largely to the bullet-trap principle, which has replaced the necessity of the infantryman to load a special round for firing the grenade. The tubular tail section of the rifle grenade, which fits over the muzzle of the rifle, contains a series of baffles. These collapse when the bullet strikes them, using its kinetic energy to launch the grenade.

In the early days the recoil forces of rifle grenades, both anti-tank and anti-personnel, were so fierce that firing from the shoulder was impossible. Therefore, the stock of the rifle had to be rested on the ground in the kneeling position or with the stock placed to the side of the infantryman's thigh when fired from the standing position. Today changes have been made to the whole range of rifle grenades, not only in effectiveness, but also in the means of launching methods. Despite these changes and advances in explosive power the rifle grenade is not universally accepted. For example, the British Army does not readily accept them, relying instead on the 51mm mortar and shoulder-fired anti-tank weapons to fulfil the roles of the rifle grenade.

The rifle grenade is used primarily by the infantry to fill the gaps in the engagement ranges left between hand grenades and light mortars. The anti-tank rifle grenade has been criticised as not carrying a large enough warhead with sufficient explosive charge to do any damage to an MBT. Whilst this is true, anti-tank rifle grenades do still serve a useful role on the battlefield, where an infantryman can use them to engage light AFVs, such as APCs and wheeled vehicles. This leads one to consider re-classifying them as anti-vehicle rifle grenades rather than the somewhat misleading title of anti-tank grenade. All anti-tank warheads fitted to anti-tank rifle grenades function on the HEAT principle, because they lack the kinetic energy to operate with any other method.

Of all the European countries using and manufacturing rifle grenades France, Belgium and Spain are among the leaders. Of these three countries, France has probably developed the range of rifle grenades the most. One typical French design of rifle grenade has a calibre of 38mm and is classified as anti-personnel/anti-vehicle, AP/AV. It can be fired from a wide range of rifles, including the FAMAS and M-16, and is 368mm in length and weighs 420g, of which 55g represents the HE content. This 38mm grenade is the smallest of its type manufactured in France, but it can be fired out to a maximum range of 400m, with a velocity of 67m/sec. Despite the relatively small size of its shaped charge warhead it will penetrate 30mm of armour at 60 degrees obliquity. Whilst this is not particularly powerful it will fragment into some 700 pieces to make it useful against light wheeled vehicles.

A 40mm calibre range of rifle grenades is also available to the French Army and includes HEAT, with a 38mm calibre warhead, and HEAT Anti-Personnel Fragmentation rounds which carry a 30mm warhead. These rounds are 391mm and 356mm in length respectively and weigh 390gm and 405gm, also. The HEAT rifle grenade is point detonating with an effective **141** range of 125m, at which distance it will penetrate between 160mm and 200mm of armour. The 40mm HEAT-APERS-FRAG rifle grenade carries a 63gm explosive charge and produces over 350 fragments, over a 15m radius, with a super-quick point detonating fuse. This round can be used against targets between 125m and 400m range and penetrate between 60mm to 80mm of armour. Both dedicated rounds can be fired from the French Army's FAMAS rifle or M-16, and have a safety arming range of 5m from point of firing. They can be used in temperatures between -40 C and +50C, which allows them to be carried and used by Rapid Deployment Forces.

The 58mm range of French-developed rifle grenades are somewhat heavier than some designs, with a greater overall length, but their lethality is increased accordingly. All rifle grenades in the 58mm range are 380mm in length with a weight of 500gm. The HEAT grenade has a combat range of 80m to 100m and will penetrate up to 350mm of steel armour at 65 degrees obliquity, which makes it comparable to some disposable anti-tank weapons. This grenade can also be used against buildings and will defeat 1000mm to 1200mm of concrete at 60 degrees obliquity. The dual-purpose 58mm Anti-Personnel/HEAT rifle grenade in this range can be used against targets up to 300m distant at a firing angle of 45 degrees. Its anti-personnel effects produce a lethality radius of 15m and its secondary HEAT charge will penetrate 70mm of armour for anti-vehicle effects.

The inherent compactness of rifle grenades and their light weight means they can be readily used by infantry deploying from helicopters, APCs and amphibious vehicles. Each man could carry several rounds in perfect safety on his personal equipment. The penetrative capabilities of the HEAT rifle grenades fall short of the effects that can be achieved with shoulder-fired anti-tank weapons, such as the AT-4. However, they do allow infantry to engage light AFVs and wheeled vehicles with quick and spontaneous response times. The Israeli Army has a range of rifle grenades available to it for use from their 5.56mm Galil rifle and includes HEAT, AP and smoke rounds. They still use ballistite cartridges to launch some types of rifle grenades and for this purpose an infantryman will carry ten rounds in a pre-loaded reserve magazine. This bears a special white band to identify the rounds as ballistite cartridges.

Rifle grenades with HEAT warheads can also be used against sandbagged machine gun emplacements or mortar pits, thereby allowing the true, more powerful anti-tank weapons to be conserved for use against a more fitting target. It is unlikely that anti-tank rifle grenades could produce either an 'M' (Mobility) or 'P' (Personnel) kill on an MBT, but against light APCs and unarmoured wheeled vehicles they are useful – particularly at shorter ranges where their accuracy is not so erratic.

The Belgians have developed a special telescopic range of rifle grenades, which at 190mm length is almost half the size of normal rifle grenades in the stored or collapsed condition. This compact design allows an infantryman to carry several rounds on his personal equipment or in a special harness. Only when it is fitted to the muzzle of the rifle ready for launching is the telescopic rifle grenade extended to 290mm length. On firing a recoil force of only 45 Joules is produced, instead of the 70 Joules to 95 Joules with normal grenades. This low recoil permits the infantryman firing the rifle grenade to aim and fire directly from the shoulder for increased accuracy. It is possible to use the telescopic rifle grenade from a wide range of rifles in either 5.56mm or 7.62mm NATO calibres.

A rifle grenade fitted to the muzzle of an infantryman's weapon does prevent him from firing in the normal way. However, rifle grenades have no backblast and can therefore be fired with complete safety from within confined spaces – including rooms of buildings that have been defensively sandbagged. This allows an infantryman to take a vehicle by surprise and fire a HEAT rifle grenade at very short ranges from elevated angles, such as upstairs windows of buildings. From this elevated vantage point he is then able to fire at vulnerable points on the AFV as it passes. Such soft points on the vehicle would include the rear engine deck or roof area on the turret, where armour is usually at its thinnest distribution. In fact, this is probably the only way in which an anti-tank rifle grenade with a HEAT warhead could incapacitate an MBT. At any other time targets would be limited to light APCs or wheeled vehicles.

Unlike shoulder-fired or guided anti-tank weapons, anti-tank rifle grenades do not have specific names for individual types, just calibres and manufacturer's names.

For this reason only a handful of the many types in service have been mentioned. All types of rifle grenade are classified as being complete rounds of ammunition and require no preparation to firing. They have an in-built safety device that arms the device only after it has been fired from the muzzle of the rifle. This allows them to be carried in perfect safety under all conditions, yet they can be brought into action against targets with only a minimum delay time whilst an infantryman fits one to the muzzle of his rifle.